The Political Ontology of
Martin Heidegger

For Marie-Claire

The Political Ontology of Martin Heidegger

Pierre Bourdieu

Translated by Peter Collier

Polity Press

Published with the assistance of the French Ministry of Culture

First published in French as *l'Ontologie politique de Martin Heidegger*
© Les Éditions de Minuit 1988

First published in paperback 1996.

Editorial office:
Polity Press, 65 Bridge Street,
Cambridge CB2 1UR, UK

Marketing and production:
Blackwell Publishers Ltd
108 Cowley Road, Oxford OX4 1JF, UK

ISBN 0 7456 0702 0
ISBN 0 7456 1714 X (pbk)

A CIP catalogue record for this book is available from the
British Library

Typeset in 11 on 13 pt Times
by Colset Private Limited, Singapore
Printed in Great Britain by T.J. Press Ltd., Padstow, Cornwall

Contents

Contents

Preface

A slightly different version of this book was first published in 1975, in *Actes de la recherche en sciences sociales*. It was devised primarily as an exercise in method, not as an accusation. Properly scientific analysis avoids the logic of litigation and cross-questioning (Was Heidegger a Nazi? Was his philosophy a Nazi philosophy? Should we teach Heidegger? etc.), so I doubt whether the unhealthy excitement surrounding this philosopher today is really propitious to a proper reception of my book, which is bound to appear as untimely now as it did on its first appearance.

The principal alteration which I have made, apart from adding some notes in order to update the historical context, has been to move the three chapters where I develop my analysis of Heidegger's language and the readings it invites, to the end of the book in order to make my argument easier to follow. I have thus taken the risk of obscuring the fact that, contrary to one widely-held view of sociology, it was a reading of the work itself, with its dual meanings and covert undertones, that revealed some of the most unexpected political implications of Heidegger's philosophy, at a time when they were not recognized by historians: its condemnation of the Welfare State, hidden deep inside a theory of temporality;

its anti-semitism, sublimated as a condemnation of rootlessness ['errance']; its refusal to disavow the commitment to
Nazism, evident in the tortuous allusions which punctuate
Heidegger's dialogue with Jünger; its ultra-revolutionary
conservatism, which inspired not only philosophical strategies
of radical overcoming but also, as Hugo Ott has shown, the
disappointed philosopher's break with the Hitler regime,
when it failed to reward his revolutionary aspirations to the
vocation of philosophical Führer.

All of this was there in the text, waiting to be read, but it was
rejected by the guardians of orthodox interpretation, who
have felt their privileges threatened by the unruly progress of
the new sciences, and so have clung like fallen aristocrats to a
philosophy of philosophy, whose exemplary expression was
provided by Heidegger, erecting a sacred barrier between
ontology and anthropology. But the best that the orthodox
can hope for is to postpone the moment when they will finally
have to agree to scrutinize the blindness of the professionals of
insight, which Heidegger manifested more clearly than any
other philosopher, and which they continue to reduplicate and
consecrate through their wilful ignorance and disdainful
silence.

Paris, January 1988

Introduction

Skewed thinking

Skewed [*louche*]. This term is used, in grammar, to indicate utterances which seem at first to introduce one meaning but which go on to articulate an entirely different one. It is used in particular of phrases whose logical construction is ambivalent to the point of disturbing their clarity of expression. What renders a phrase *skewed* arises therefore in the specific disposition of the words which compose it, when they seem at first glance to create a certain relation, although in fact they entertain a different one: just as *skew-eyed* people seem to look in one direction, while they are actually looking somewhere else.

M. Beauzée, *Encyclopédie méthodique, grammaire et littérature.*

There are doubtless few intellectual systems more profoundly rooted in and dated by their times than what Croce called the 'pure philosophy' of Heidegger.[1] There are no contemporary problems, nor ideological responses by the 'conservative revolutionaries' to these problems, which are not present in this absolute work, however sublimated and misleading their form. And yet there are few works which have been read in such a profoundly ahistorical way. Not even the most ruthless investigators into the author of *Sein und Zeit*'s murky compromises with Nazism have looked at the texts themselves for indices, admissions, or hints liable to reveal or elucidate the political commitment of its author.

Yet it would be futile to try to convince people of this constant, universal reference to the historical situation and the cultural context, by comparing Heidegger's thought for instance to those kinds of less artfully euphemized discourse which are its equivalent, *except that they belong to a different system*. The relative autonomy of the field of philosophical production means that such a comparison may serve *just as easily* to prove dependence as independence. Paradoxically, the 'field' effect, that is the effect operated on the production of philosophical discourse by the specific constraints of the philosophical microcosm, is just what gives an objective basis to the illusion of absolute autonomy. This effect can be invoked to prohibit or reject *a priori* any comparison of the work of Heidegger, a conservative revolutionary *in philosophy* (that is, in the relatively autonomous field of philosophy), with the works of economists like Sombart and Spann or political essayists like Spengler or Jünger, who would appear to be temptingly similar to Heidegger, if this were not precisely the kind of case where it is impossible to argue in terms of 'other things being equal'. Any adequate analysis must accommodate a dual refusal, rejecting not only any claim of the philosophical text to absolute autonomy, with its concomitant rejection of all external reference, but also any direct reduction of the text to the most general conditions of its production. We may recognize its independence, but on condition that we openly admit that this is only another name for dependence on the specific rules governing the internal functioning of the philosophical field; we may recognize its dependence, but on condition that we take account of the systematic transformations to which the effects of this dependence are subject, since it is only ever exercised through the medium of mechanisms specific to the philosophical field.

Thus we must abandon the opposition between a political reading and a philosophical reading, and undertake a simultaneously political and philosophical *dual reading* of writings which are defined by their fundamental *ambiguity*, that is, by their reference to two social spaces, which correspond to two mental spaces. Because he overlooks the relative autonomy of the philosophical field, Adorno relates the pertinent features of Heidegger's philosophy to characteristics of the class fraction to which Heidegger belongs. This 'short-circuit' leads Adorno to interpret his nostalgic ideology as the expression of a group of intellectuals who lack economic independence and power and are out of their depth in industrial society. I have no desire to challenge this connection, any more than another connection which Adorno establishes, between the themes of 'anxiety' or 'absurdity' and the practical impotence of the authors of these themes – especially in the light of Ringer's book, which relates the increasingly reactionary conservatism of those he calls the 'German mandarins' to their declining position within the structure of the dominant class. However, since Adorno is unable to grasp the decisive mediation represented by the positions which constitute the philosophical field and their relation to the founding oppositions of the philosophical system, he inevitably fails to reveal the alchemical transformation which protects philosophical discourse from direct reduction to the class position of its producer. Adorno thereby blinds himself to what we might expect to find most crucial, namely, the imposition of form that is effected by philosophical discourse.

Whether they are opponents who reject his philosophy in the name of its affiliation to Nazism or apologists who separate the philosophy from its author's sympathy for Nazism, all the critics contrive to ignore the fact that Heidegger's philosophy might be only a sublimated philosophical version, imposed by the forms of censorship specific to the field of philosophical production, of the political or ethical principles which determined the philosopher's support for Nazism. Through their obstinacy in concentrating on biographical facts without relating them to the internal logic of his writing, Heidegger's opponents concede to his supporters the right to claim an explicit distinction between the 'critical establishment of the facts' and 'textual hermeneutics'.[2] On the one hand we have Heidegger's biography, with its public and private events – his birth on 26 September 1889 into a family of small craftsmen in a little Black Forest village, his primary education at Messkirch, secondary studies at Constance and Freiburg-in-Brisgau, then, in 1909, higher education at the University of Freiburg, where he took courses in philosophy and theology, his doctorate in philosophy in 1913, and so on, with, in passing, membership of the Nazi party, the Rectoral address, and some silences. On the other hand, we have the intellectual biography, 'laundered' of all reference to events in the everyday life of the philosopher. In this area, the 'Verzeichnis der Vorlesungen und Uebungen von Martin Heidegger', an inventory of Heidegger's teaching from 1915 to 1958, is an exemplary document. When he is reduced to the only temporal practice deemed legitimate, teaching philosophy, and even then only to the public face of this teaching,[3] the thinker becomes completely identified with his thought, and his life with his work – which is thus constituted as a self-sufficient and self-generating creation.

And yet the most reductive critics cannot help being struck by the presence, even in the most directly political writings,[4] of a certain vocabulary typical of Heidegger's philosophical idiolect (*Wesen des Seins* [the essence of Being], *menschliches Dasein* [human existence], *Wesenswille* [the will to be], *Geschick* [fate], *Verlassenheit* [dereliction], etc.) alongside the typically Nazi vocabulary and the 'reminiscences of editorials in the *Völkische Beobachter* and speeches by Goebbels'.[5] It is significant that the Rectoral address of 27 May 1933, entitled 'The Defence (*Selbstbehauptung*, sometimes pompously overtranslated as self-assertion or self-affirmation) of the University', which has so often been invoked to demonstrate Heidegger's support for Nazism, can find its place even in such a pure and purely internal history of Heidegger's thought as that written by Richardson.[6] No doubt the author of this expurgated history went to considerable lengths to endow a circumstantial posture with the appearance of an entirely consequential application (in Gadamer's sense) of philosophical theory (with, for instance, its attack on objective science). But Karl Löwith himself explains clearly enough the ambiguity of this text: 'Compared with the countless pamphlets and speeches published after the fall of the Weimar regime by professors who had been "brought into line", Heidegger's speech has an extremely philosophical and demanding tone; it is a minor masterpiece of expression and composition. Measured by philosophical standards, his discourse is from beginning to end of a rare ambiguity, for it manages to subordinate existential and ontological categories to the historical "moment" so that they create the illusion that their philosophical intentions have an *a priori* applicability to the political situation, as when he relates freedom of research to State coercion, and makes "labour service" and "armed service" coincide with "knowledge service", so that by the end of the lecture the listener does not know whether to turn to read Diels on "the pre-Socratics" or join the S. A. That is why one cannot simply judge this speech from one point of view, whether purely political, or purely philosophical.'[7]

It is just as wrong to situate Heidegger in the purely political arena, relying on the affinity of his thought to that of essayists like Spengler or Jünger, as it is to localize him in the 'philosophical' arena 'properly speaking', that is in the relatively autonomous history of philosophy, for instance in the name of his opposition to the neo-Kantians. The most specific characteristics and effects of his thought are rooted in this dual reference, and in order to understand it adequately, we must ourselves regenerate, consciously and methodically, the reciprocal connections that Heidegger's political ontology sets up in practice, as it creates a political stance but gives it a purely philosophical expression.

The best chance of any specialized discourse resisting objectification lies, as we can see, in the enormity of the task involved in revealing the complete system of relations which informs it. Thus, in the present case, our task should be no less than to reconstruct the structure of the field of philosophical production – including the whole of its previous historical development – as well as the structure of the university field, which assigns the body of philosophers to their 'site' (as Heidegger would say) and their functions. We ought also to reconstruct the structure of the field of power, where the places of the professors and their opportunities are defined, and thus, step by step, the whole social structure of Weimar Germany.[8] We have only to judge the scale of this enterprise to see that a scientific analysis is doomed to attract the combined criticism of the guardians of form, who deem sacrilegious or vulgar any approach straying from an internal meditation on the work, and the criticism of those who, knowing in advance what they should think 'in the last analysis', will automatically adjust their *theoretical* positions to suit the result of their own analyses, in order to denounce the inevitable limitations of any *practical* analysis.[9]

1

Pure philosophy and the *Zeitgeist*

When Heidegger addresses 'our thought-provoking time' (*in unserer bedenklichen Zeit*), we recognize a Nietzschean tone. We should take him at his word, as we should when he talks of 'the thought-provoking' (*das Bedenkliche*) or 'the most thought-provoking' (*das Bedenklichste*).[1] Although he adopts a prophetic posture ('we do not yet think', etc.), Heidegger is right to affirm that his thinking reflects a critical moment, or what he also calls an *Umsturzsituation*, a 'revolutionary situation'. In his own way, he never ceased to reflect on the profound crisis of which Germany was the focus; or rather, to be more precise, the crisis of Germany and the German university system never ceased to be reflected and expressed through him. The crisis comprised the First World War and the (incomplete) revolution of November 1918, which spelled out the possibility of a Bolshevik revolution and struck lasting fear into the hearts of the conservatives, at the same time as profoundly disappointing the writers and artists (Rilke and Brecht, for instance) once their moment of enthusiasm had passed;[2] the political assassinations (whose perpetrators often went unpunished); Kapp's putsch and other attempts at subversion; the defeat; the Treaty of Versailles; the occupation of the Ruhr by the French and the territorial amputations which exacerbated people's awareness of *Deutschtum* as a community of language and blood; the galloping inflation of 1919-24, which affected above all the *Mittelstand* [the middle classes]; the brief period of *Prosperität* [prosperity], which introduced an obsession with technology and the rationalization of labour; and finally the great depression of 1929. All these events helped to create a traumatic experience, which was bound to have a permanent impact, albeit to different degrees and with different effects, on the vision of the social world held by a whole generation of intellectuals. These experiences found a more or less euphemized expression in endless speeches on 'the age of the masses' and on 'technology', as much as in expressionist painting, poetry, and cinema, and in that paroxysmic and passionate finale to a movement – commonly known as 'Weimar Culture' – which was born in *fin-de-siècle* Vienna, haunted by the 'discontents of civilization', fascinated by war and death, and revolted by technological civilization as well as by all forms of authority.

This is the context in which there developed, at first on the margins of the university, an entirely distinctive *ideological mood*, which gradually impregnated the whole of the educated bourgeoisie. It is difficult to say whether this metaphysico-political vulgate was a popularized version of learned economic and philosophical theories, or whether it was the outcome of an independent process of spontaneous regeneration. However, one factor which inclines us to believe in a process of 'popularization' is the fact that we find a whole range of expressions which fulfil equivalent functions, but at gradually less demanding degrees of *formal* rigour, that is, of euphemization and rationalization. Spengler, who seems to be a 'popularizer' of Sombart and of Spann, appears in his turn to be 'popularized' by the students and the young teachers of the 'youth movement', who call for an end to 'alienation' – one of the key words of the period, but used as a synonym for 'uprooting' – by seeking 're-rooting' in the homeland, the people, and nature (with forest walks and mountain treks).

The youth movement denounces the tyranny of reason and the intellect for spurning the friendly voices of nature, and preaches a return to culture and *inwardness*, entailing a rejection of the vulgar, material, bourgeois pursuit of comfort and profit. But the current also flows in the other direction.

This confused, synchretistic language is merely the pale, unfocused objectification of a collective *Stimmung* [mood] whose spokesmen are themselves only echoes. This *völkisch* [populist] mood is fundamentally a disposition towards the world which remains irreducible to all objectification in speech or in any other form of expression. It may be recognized in a bodily *hexis*, in a relation to language, and also, but this is not essential, in a series of literary and philosophical mentors (Kierkegaard, Dostoevsky, Tolstoy, Nietzsche) and politico-metaphysico-moral arguments. But we must not allow our search for distant origins to deflect our bearings: clearly, as early as the nineteenth century we may find Paul de Lagarde (born in 1827), Julius Langbehn (born in 1851) and, nearer to us, Othmar Spann (born in 1878), who continued the work of Adam Müller, or Diederichs, the editor of *Die Tat*, whose 'new Romanticism' exercised an enormous influence until his death in 1927. But we should not ignore the historians whose vision of the ancient Germanic people is dominated by the racist theory that Houston Stewart Chamberlain drew from his reading of Tacitus' *Germania*; the *völkisch* novel and *Blubo-Literatur* (from *Blut und Boden*, blood and earth) with its glorification of provincial life, nature, and the return to nature; esoteric circles such as the 'cosmics' of Klages and Schuler and every imaginable kind of search for spiritual experience. Nor should we forget the *Bayreuther Blätter*, the anti-semitic journal of a heroic and purified Wagnerian Germany, and the great productions of the national theatre; the racist biology and philology of Aryanism and Carl Schmitt's brand of law; teaching, including the outlet provided by school textbooks for the expression of *völkisch* ideology, and, in particular, for so-called *Heimatkunde*, the

lore of the homeland.³ These countless 'sources', springing up
on all sides, provide the fundamental properties of an ideological configuration which is composed of words used as
exclamations of ecstasy or indignation, and of semi-scholarly
topics newly adapted. These 'spontaneously' produced personal ideas are objectively orchestrated, because they are
grounded in an orchestration of the *habitus* and an affective
harmony of shared phantasms, which give them at one and
the same time the appearance of unity and yet of unlimited
originality.

But the *völkisch* mood is also a set of questions through
which the whole period offers itself up as matter for reflection:
these questions, which are as vague as states of mind, but as
powerful and obsessive as phantasms, are concerned with
technology, the workers, the elite, history, and the homeland.
It is hardly surprising, then, if this pathos-ridden enquiry finds
its privileged expression in the cinema, in, for example, the
crowd scenes of Lubitsch, the queues in the films of Pabst
(paradigmatic representations of *Das Man* [Heidegger's anonymous 'they']), or that virtual summary of all their fantasized
problematics, Fritz Lang's *Metropolis*,⁴ a graphic retranslation of Jünger's *Der Arbeiter* (*The Worker*).⁵

Because of its uncertain, syncretistic nature, which strains
rational expression to its limits, *völkisch* ideology found its
best expression in literature and above all the cinema. In this
respect, Siegfried Krakauer's book, *From Caligari to Hitler, a
Psychological History of the German Cinema*,⁶ is no doubt
one of the best evocations of the spirit of the times. Apart from
the obsessive presence of the street and the masses (*passim*), we
should note in particular topics like that of 'patriarchal abso-
lutism' in *Ein Glas Wasser* (A Glass of Water) and *Der
Verlorene Schuh* (Cinderella), two films by Ludwig Berger
which envisaged 'a better future' in terms of a return to the
good old days (p. 108), and that of the 'inner metamorphosis
(*innere Wandlung*) which counts more than any transformation of the outer world' (p. 108). This was one of the topics

dearest to the hearts of the German petty bourgeoisie, as witness the extraordinary contemporary success of Dostoevsky,
in Möller van den Bruck's translation.[7] Finally, another topic
that became extraordinarily successful was 'the mountain',
which gave birth to an 'exclusively German' genre. This
includes, among others, all the films of Dr Arnold Franck,
who specialized in this 'mixture of sparkling ice-axes and
inflated sentiments'. In fact, as Siegfried Krakauer notes, 'the
message of the mountains that Franck endeavoured to popu-
larize through such splendid shots was the credo of many Germans with academic titles, and some without, including a part
of the university youth. Long before the First World War,
groups of Munich students left the dull capital every weekend
for the nearby Bavarian Alps, and they indulged their pas-
sion. . . . Full of Promethean promptings, they would climb
up some dangerous "chimney", then quietly smoke their pipes
on the summit, and with infinite pride look down on what they
called "valley pigs" – those plebeian crowds who never made
an effort to elevate themselves to lofty heights' (p. 111).

Spengler, who was well placed to detect and even predict
this change in collective mood, gives an accurate evocation of
the ideological atmosphere: 'The Faustian thought begins to
be *sick* of machines. A weariness is spreading, a sort of
pacifism of the battle with Nature. Men are returning to forms
of life *simpler* and *nearer to Nature*; they are spending their
time in sport instead of technical experiments. The *great cities*
are becoming hateful to them, and they would fain get away
from the pressure of *soulless facts* and the clear cold atmosphere of technical organization. And it is precisely the strong
and creative talents that are turning away from *practical problems* and *sciences* and towards *pure speculation. Occultism*
and *Spiritualism, Hindu philosophies, metaphysical inquisi-
tiveness* under Christian or pagan colouring, all of which were
despised in the Darwinian period, are coming up again. It is
the spirit of Rome in the Age of Augustus. Out of the satiety of
life, men take refuge from *civilization* in the more primitive

parts of the earth, in vagabondage, in suicide'.[8] And Ernst Troeltsch shows the same overall insight into this system of attitudes, from a much more distant, and thus much more objective, viewpoint, in an article published in 1921 where he sketches the main features of the *Jugendbewegung*: the rejection of exercise and discipline, of the ideology of success and power, of the cumbersome but superficial education suffered at school, of intellectualism and literary complacency, of the 'metropolitan' and the artificial, of materialism and scepticism, of authoritarianism and the reign of money and prestige. In addition he records people's hopes for 'a synthesis, a system, a *Weltanschauung* and value judgements', a need for renewed spontaneity and inwardness, for a new intellectual and spiritual aristocracy to counter rationalism and the democratic levelling-down and spiritual vacuity of Marxism. He also records hostility towards the mathematization and the mechanization of all European philosophy since Galileo and Descartes, as well as recording attacks on evolutionist theories and critical awareness, on precise methodology and rigorous analysis or research.[9]

The *völkisch* language, a 'literate' message intended for a 'literate and cultured' audience,[10] kept cropping up here and there on the fringes of the university system, in fashionable circles or arty-intellectual groups; then it took root in the universities, at first among the students and junior teachers, until, at the end of a complex dialectical process, of which Heidegger's work was one stage, it flourished among the professors themselves. The effect of economic and political events was mediated through the crisis specific to the university field, which was determined by the following: the influx of students[11] and the uncertainty of career opportunities; the emergence of a university proletariat condemned either to 'teach below the university level', or to live from hand to mouth on the fringes of the university system (as in the case of Hitler's spiritual master, D. Eckart, impoverished editor of a small Munich review, *Auf gut Deutsch*); and the decline, through inflation, of the economic and social status of the professors, often inclined to adopt conservative and national-ist or even xenophobic and anti-semitic stances.[12] To which we should add the effect of the demand for a more practical edu-cation, addressed to the universities by the State and heavy industry, albeit with different expectations and intentions, as well as criticism from the political parties who included educational reform in their manifestos after 1919, and who protested at the intellectually and spiritually aristocratic tradi-tions of the universities.[13]

The 'academic proletarians', that is, the 'men who had received their doctorate but who were compelled to teach below the university level because of the scarcity of profes-sorial chairs'[14] and the 'young academic workers' who pro-liferated as a result of the great scientific institutes becoming '"state capitalist" enterprises',[15] was swollen with all those everlasting students that the logic of the German university system allowed to stagnate in junior teaching positions. Thus there was, at the heart of the university system itself, a 'free intelligentsia' which under a stricter regime would have been banished to the literary cafés: these intellectuals, literally torn by the contrast between the spiritual rewards and the material stipend offered by the university, were predisposed to play the part of an *avant-garde*, detecting and proclaiming the com-mon fate awaiting a university corps whose economic and symbolic privileges are doomed.[16]

It is hardly surprising that what was then known as the 'crisis of the university' was accompanied by what Aloys Fischer calls a 'crisis of the authorities' and a redefinition of the bases of professorial authority: anti-intellectualism, like all forms of mystical or spiritualist irrationalism, is always a satisfying way of challenging the academic tribunal and its verdicts. But the anti-intellectualism of the students and the junior teachers whose future seemed threatened could not itself lead to a profound questioning of the educational establishment, since, as Fischer remarks, it attacked all the

intellectual traditions which had already been discredited by
the professors themselves: naturalist positivism, utilitarianism, etc.[17] The objective decline of the relative position
of the professorial body, and the specific crisis which had
affected the 'arts faculties' since the end of the nineteenth
century (with the progress of the natural sciences and the
social sciences, and the concomitant reversal of academic
hierarchies), was bound to encourage university professors to
join those who lamented the decline of Western culture or
civilization. The conservative indignation which welled up
after 1918 in the bosom of the German university, and which
thrived on slogans and clichés attacking 'individualism' (or
'selfishness') and indicting 'utilitarian and materialistic
tendencies' and the crisis of knowledge (*Krise der Wissenschaft*), etc., owed its politically conservative and antidemocratic colouring to the fact that it was developed in
response to attacks launched by the parties of the left (and
relayed, at least partly, by the social sciences, especially
sociology) against the academic norms and the intellectually
aristocratic ideas of the German universities. Fritz Ringer
records all the terms which functioned as crude emotional
stimuli and triggered an entire political world-view: for
example 'disintegration' (*Zersetzung*) or 'decomposition'
(*Dekomposition*) evoked not only the weakening of natural,
irrational, or moral bonds between men in an 'industrial
society', but also the purely intellectual techniques which had
helped to destroy the traditional bases of social cohesion by
submitting them to a critical analysis. He gives copious quota-
tions from the antimodernist, antipositivist, antiscientific,
antidemocratic, etc., statements promulgated by German professors in response to the crisis, not of culture, as they argued,
but of their own cultural capital.

> 'We are surrounded on all sides by the destructive and the
> low-mindedly iconoclastic, the arbitrary and the formless, the
> levelling and mechanizing of this machine age, the methodical
> dissolution of everything that is healthy and noble, the

ridiculing of everything strong and serious, the dishonouring of everything godly, which lifts men up in that they serve it'.[18] 'As the masses plod along the daily treadmill of their lives like slaves or automatons, soullessly, thoughtlessly, and mechanically . . ., all events in nature and in society appear shallowly mechanized to their technicized and routinized manner of thinking. Everything, they believe, . . . is as mediocre and average as the mass products of the factory; everything is the same and can be distinguished only by number. There are, they think, no differences between races, peoples, and states, no hierarchy of talent and achievement, no superiority of one over the other, and where living standards are still different in fact, they seek – envious of nobility of birth, education, and culture, to create a fully equal place'.[19]

When the professional thinker believes himself to be directly conceptualizing the social world, his thoughts are none the less inevitably channelled through something that has already been thought, and this obtains as much for the journal (which appealed to Hegel), or the fashionable pamphlet written by a political journalist as it does for the works of his professional colleagues; they all describe the same social world, of course, but they all use more or less sophisticated systems of euphemisms to describe it. The discourse of academics like Werner Sombart, Edgar Salin, Carl Schmitt, or Othmar Spann, or essay writers like Möller van den Bruck, Oswald Spengler, Ernst Jünger, or Ernst Niekisch, and the countless variants of 'conservative ideology' which the German professors produced every day in their lectures, offered Heidegger, as he did for them and as they did for each other, food for thought, but of a very specific kind, since (despite their different thought-patterns and modes of expression) they provided an objectification which echoed his own politico-moral moods.

If we wished to demonstrate all the intricate connections of these thematic and lexical ramifications, which provide each other with mutual reinforcement, we would have to quote wholesale from every work written by those writers who were the mouthpieces of the *Zeitgeist*, who acted as spokesmen for the whole group and helped decisively to shape mental structures by creating a highly successful objectification of communal dispositions. One thinks especially of Spengler: his little book *Man and Technics*, written in 1931, condensed the ideological substance of *The Decline of the West*, which, after the publication of its first volume in 1918 and its second in 1922, had become a universal point of reference.

Spengler's denunciation of the 'plebeian theory of rationalism, liberalism, and socialism' (*Man and Technics*, p. 80) finds its focus in a critique of 'trivial optimism' (p. 7), of faith in technical progress (p. 12), and 'rose-coloured progress – optimism', described in quasi-Heideggerian terms as a flight from the truth of human existence as 'birth', 'decay', and 'the ephemeral' (pp. 13–14). Significantly, it is in this context that Spengler develops, albeit in rudimentary form, the themes of the resolute consciousness of death (p. 14) and of care 'that presupposes mental vision into the future, concern for what *is to be*' (p. 30), seeing them as the distinctive features of the human being. His critique of science (seen as a Faustian 'myth', but one which has then become founded on 'a working hypothesis' which 'aims, not at embracing and unveiling the secrets of the world, but at making them serviceable to definite ends' (p. 82)), and the *diabolical* will to dominate nature, which lead to a 'belief in technics' which is tantamount to a 'materialistic religion' (p. 86), culminates in the apocalyptic evocation (announced by the Heidegger of 'The Essence of the Technical') of the domination of man by the technical, of the 'mechanization of the world' (p. 93) and of the reign of the 'artificial' (p. 88) – the antithesis of 'the beautiful old handwork of an unspoilt primitive people' (p. 94): 'All things organic are dying in the grip of the vice of organization. An artificial world is permeating and poisoning the natural. The civilization itself has become a machine that does, or tries to do, everything in mechanical fashion. We think only in horse-power now; we cannot look at a waterfall without mentally turning it into electric power' (p. 94).

This central theme is intertwined, without apparent logic, with a brutal apologia, verging on racism (pp. 67, 100-3), for the 'natural divisions' which 'distinguish the strong from the weak and the clever from the stupid' (p. 76), with an unvarnished affirmation of the 'natural distinction of grade' (p. 64) founded in biology, like the contrast between the lion and the cow (p. 25), as evident in 'every zoological garden' (p. 26), and the 'genius' or 'talent' (p. 64) of the 'born leader' (p. 97), the 'beast of prey', and the 'highly gifted' (p. 93) as opposed to the 'superfluous and forlorn herd', the 'mass', which 'is no more than a negation' (p. 99), a residue of inevitably envious, sub-human people (pp. 71-2). The connection, suggested by their parallel deployment, between the 'ecological' theme of the 'return to nature' (p. 69) and the hierarchical theme of the 'natural law' (p. 66) depends no doubt on a sort of phantasmatic manipulation of the notion of *nature*: the ideological exploitation of a nostalgia for the countryside and a malaise in urban civilization relies on a surreptitious identification of the return to nature with a return to natural law, which can operate through different channels, such as a revival of magical relations of a paternalist or patriarchal type, associated with the world of the peasant, or, more crudely, an appeal to the differences and the drives universally inherent in nature (and particularly in *animal* nature).

We find these two focal topics connected, more or less randomly according to the drift of the argument, with sociologically related topics, such as a condemnation of the 'completely anti-natural' city and the totally artificial social divisions which are developed there (p. 76); a denunciation of the domination of life and the soul, and the life of the soul, by thought, reason, and the intellect; an appreciation of 'physiognomic tact', the global, totalizing approach which alone can secure the unity of 'life' against all analytic compartmentalization (p. 8).

The political truth of these would-be philosophical opinions was revealed in literal form in *Preussentum und Sozialismus*, an overtly political pamphlet published in 1920, which failed to damage the reputation for profound thinking that the

author of *The Decline of the West* had acquired among even
the academic community. In it Spengler develops a theory of
'Prussian socialism' which he opposes to 'English socialism',
which is materialist, cosmopolitan, and liberal: the Germans
should go back to the tradition of authoritarian socialism of
Frederick II's times, whose essence was antiliberal and antidemocratic, and gave precedence to the totality over the individual, born to obey. Spengler sees traces of this tradition even
in Bebel's German socialist party and its 'batallions of
workers', with their military sense of discipline and calm resolution, and their readiness to die courageously in the name of
superior values.

In order to give a properly genetic account of the logic of the
production of this discourse, we can look at Ernst Jünger, for
whom Heidegger frequently demonstrated the greatest intellectual esteem. Jünger, inspired by the freedom enjoyed by
genres like the journal or the novel, which authorize and
encourage cultivation of the unique or 'rare experience',
offers up his unmediated reactions to 'primitive situations':
and here we may find the roots of the essay-writer's *primal
phantasms*, the hidden principles of his often laborious
constructions.[20]

'With Friedrich Georg . . . at the zoo, *on this half-price Sun-
day*. The sight of the *masses* is extremely oppressive, but we
must not forget that we see them in the cold light of statistics'
(E. Jünger, *Gärten und Strassen*, in *Werke*, vol. 2, p. 64; my
emphasis). 'Two days in Hamburg. Even when we visit *big
cities* regularly, we are struck each time by the aggravation of
their *automatic* character' (p. 68). 'The *spectators leaving the
cinema* look like a *sleeping crowd* just waking up, and, when
we go into *rooms overflowing with mechanical music*, we have
a feeling rather like that of entering the atmosphere of an
opium den' (p. 69). 'All the *antennae of these giant cities* seem
like so many hairs of the head standing up on end. They solicit
a *satanic* complicity' (Jünger, *Der Waldgang*, in *Werke*,
vol. 5, p. 321). All we need now is an appeal for situations

where elite souls can feel their distinction: 'The non-smoking compartments are always less crowded than the others; *asceticism*, even in its lesser manifestations, gives a man *breathing space*' (*Gärten und Strassen*, p. 101).

Now that we are forearmed with an inkling of the vision of the social world held by this 'conservative anarchist', this hero of the Great War brought up on Sorel and Spengler,[21] who will extol war, technology and 'total mobilization' and will seek an authentically German conception of freedom not in the principles of the *Aufklärung* [Enlightenment] but in a 'German' responsibility and a 'German' order,[22] who will denounce rationalism and the bourgeois desire for security in order to celebrate an art of living conceived as an art of fighting and dying, we may now confront his 'social philosophy' as it is expressed in the *Der Waldgang* [*Treatise of the Rebel*],[23] a less ambitious and more transparent formulation of the theses of *The Worker*. This work is organized around a set of alternatives which focus on the antithesis between the Worker, whom allegory renders ostensibly heroic, and the Rebel: the former obeys the 'technical principle'; he is reduced by the technical, the collective, and the typical to a fully automatic state; he is a slave to technology and science, comfort and 'stimuli received',[24] in short, he is indiscriminate man, a 'number' whose mechanical, purely statistical multiplication produces 'the masses', that is, the 'collective powers' of the 'lower depths', which the era of subsidized transport allows to flood into areas previously reserved.[25] Confronting this negative product of all the determinisms of 'the technicians' civilization' is 'the Rebel'[26] – the poet, the unique individual, the leader – whose (lofty, sublime, etc.) 'realm' is 'that place of freedom' 'known as the forest'. The 'search for the forest', 'a dangerous path which leads not only *beyond the beaten track*, but also beyond the frontiers of meditation'[27] – and how can we avoid thinking of *Holzwege*? – promises a return to the 'native land', to our 'sources' and 'roots', to 'myth' and

'mystery', to the 'sacred' and the 'secret',[28] to the wisdom of
the simple, in short, to the 'original strength' which belongs
to the man who 'enjoys danger' and prefers death to base
servitude.[29] On the one hand, then, we have the 'world of
social security',[30] of equality, collectivity, and down-levelling
socialism,[31] a universe several times labelled 'zoological';[32] on
the other hand, the realm reserved for 'a tiny elite',[33] who do
not reject the fraternity of the 'simple' and the 'humble'.[34]
Thus the remedy to which Jünger turns is a *return*,[35] and we
understand why this vision of the social world is resumed in a
philosophy of temporality which opposes linear, forward-
moving, and 'progressive' time (leading towards the ultimate
'catastrophe' of the technical world), in the name of a cyclical
time (which 'turns back' the clock) that is the perfect symbol
of the *conservative revolution*, of the *Restoration*, as a denial
of revolution.[36]

Faced with an ideological universe so monotonous that it is
often very difficult to tell the difference between the various
authors – especially the most popular ones – the first natural
reaction for the professional intellectual, who is inevitably
imbued with structuralist habits, is to draw up a 'table' of the
pertinent oppositions, for each author as well as for the set of
related authors. In fact the effect of such a formal construction would be to destroy the specific logic of these ideological
clusters, which is articulated on the level of patterns of production, rather than that of the products themselves. The
specific feature of the topoi which give an objective unity to
the expressions of a whole era is their quasi-indeterminate
nature, which makes them akin to the fundamental polarities
that structure mythical systems: there is little doubt that
if we record all the uses of the opposition between culture
(*Kultur*) and civilization (*Zivilisation*), the intersection is more
or less empty;[37] but this does not prevent a practical grasp of
that distinction from giving us a working sense of ethical and
political orientation, which enables us in any particular case
to produce loose, general definitions which are never entirely

interchangeable with those of another user, nor entirely different, and which thereby confer on all the expressions of the period that air of unity which defies logical analysis but which constitutes one of the important elements of a sociological definition of contemporaneity. Thus it is that culture, for Spengler, is opposed to civilization, 'the most artificial and superficial state of which humanity is capable', as the dynamic is to the static, the becoming to the dead and gone (*rigor mortis*), the internal to the external, the organic to the mechanical, the naturally developing to the artificially constructed, the ends to the means, the soul, life, and instinct to reason and decadence. These binary oppositions only obtain, as we see, by buttressing each other like a stack of cards, through very vaguely defined analogies. We have only to try to take out one of them on its own for the whole edifice to collapse. Each thinker produces his own series, derived from the crude mental schemata and the corresponding practical options which they generate:[38] by using the generative contradiction either in its primary form, like Spengler, or in a more elaborate, often barely recognizable, form, like Heidegger, who replaces it, while granting it the same function, with the contrast between 'essential thought' and the sciences. Thus a given thinker may, in a particular situation or context, develop applications which would seem contrary to rigorous logic, yet may be justified in terms of the logic which matches the pairs of practical contradictions that found the partial systematizations.

The unifying principle of the *Zeitgeist* is the common ideological matrix, the system of common mental schemata which, behind their appearance of infinite diversity, engender the commonplaces, the sets of roughly corresponding fundamental polarities which structure people's thoughts and organize their vision of the world. These are, to mention only the most important, the oppositions between culture and civilization, between Germany and France (or, in another context, England), as a paradigm of cosmopolitanism; between

the 'community' (Tonnies's *Gemeinschaft*), and the 'people'
(*Volk*) or the incoherent masses; between the *Führer* or the
Reich and liberalism, parliamentarianism, or pacifism;
between the country or the forest and the town or the factory;
between the peasant or the hero and the worker or the shop-
keeper; between life or the organism (*Organismus*) and technology or the dehumanizing machine; between the total and
the partial or the disconnected; between integration and fragmentation;[39] between ontology and science, or godless rationalism, etc.

These choices, and the debates they occasion, are not the
sole prerogative of the conservative ideologues. They are
written into the very structure of the field of ideological production, where the problematic shared by all the thinkers of
the age is engendered in and through the antagonistic positions which go to make up the structure. As Herman Lebovics
notes, the sub-field constituted by the conservative ideologues
has a right, represented by Spengler, and a left, or rather, a far
right, represented, in two different guises which are at once
close and antithetical, by Niekisch and Jünger. Both right and
left of this conservative sub-field are enclosed within the wider
field of ideological production; and its products, as witness
the constant reference to liberalism and socialism, are (at least
negatively) marked by the effect of belonging to it. Thus
the conservatives' pessimism on the subject of technology,
science, and 'technological' civilization, etc., is the structurally
required counterpart of the *optimism* which Meyer Schapiro
identifies with the 'reformist illusion, which was especially
widespread in the brief period of post-war prosperity . . . that
the technological advance, in raising the living standards of
the people, in lowering the costs of housing and other necessities, would resolve the conflict of classes, or at any rate form in
the technicians habits of efficient economic planning, con-
ducive to a peaceful transition to socialism'.[40] And, more
generally, the 'philosophy' of the conservative revolutionaries
is defined in an essentially negative manner, as an 'ideological

attack on the . . . complex of ideas and institutions that characterize our liberal, secular, and industrial civilization'.[41] This philosophy can be derived, like a print from a negative, from the properties of its opponents: the francophiles, Jews, progressives, democrats, rationalists, socialists, cosmopolitans, and left-wing intellectuals (epitomized by Heine), seem to cry out for negation in a nationalist ideology which aimed at 'the revival of a mythical *Deutschtum* and the creation of political institutions that would embody and preserve this peculiar character of the Germans'.[42]

If the debates between those thinkers, who were bound to refer to the same space of possibilities and whose minds were often structured by the same polarities, do not degenerate into the total confusion that a retrospective view, ignoring contemporary subtleties and nuances, might lead us to infer, it is because production and reception are always guided by a politico-moral sense of orientation which, especially in a period of crisis aggravated by a university crisis, endows every word and topic – even those apparently least relevant to politics, like the question of quantification in the sciences or the problem of the role of *Erlebnis* [personal experience] in scientific knowledge – with an unambiguous place in the ideological field, that is, generally speaking, on the left or the right, for or against modernism, socialism, liberalism, or conservatism.

Sombart, like all the conservatives who adopt a position on the question of quantification (an example would be Spann, with his concept of *Ganzheit*), argues in favour of synthesis and the totality, and thus attacks 'Western' (that is French and English) sociology, as well as everything that constitutes its 'naturalism', that is 'quantification', 'mathematization', and the quest for mechanical laws. He believes that this form of knowledge, whose frigid inability to accede to the essence of Being (*Wesen*) he deplores (especially when it extends to the territory of the spirit [*Geist*]), and which he opposes to 'humanist' (that is German), sociology, reflects the development of the natural sciences and the 'disintegration' (*Zersetzung*) of European culture, that is, secularization and urbanization. It also encourages a technological approach to knowledge, the development of individualism, and the disappearance of the traditional 'community'. As we have seen, the practical syntheses effected by social perception are able to capture the quite organic coherence of a whole set of terms which at first seem unrelated. And this coherence, which suggests the presence of a whole semantic constellation in each individual element, explains the occurrence of suspicions or denunciations apparently disproportionate to their object, such as Weber's warning against those 'idols whose cult today occupies a broad place on all street corners and in all periodicals', that is, 'personality' and 'personal experience' [*Erlebnis*].[43]

Similarly, the key words of Jünger's work,[44] *Gestalt*, *Typus*, *organische Konstruktion*, *total*, *Totalität*, *Ganzheit*, *Rangordnung*, *elementar*, *innen*, are sufficient to situate it for anyone who knows their way around the field. The totality (*Gestalt*, *total*, *Totalität*, *Ganzheit*) – that is, whatever can only be apprehended intuitively (*anschaulich*), which is irreducible to the sum of its parts (as opposed to the 'cumulative'), and which, ultimately, cannot be divided up into parts but is composed of 'members' integrated into a single meaningful unit – is opposed to concepts immediately suspected of positivism, such as sum, aggregate, mechanism, analysis, and even synthesis, which Rheinhold Seeberg accused of giving the impression that reality is fragmented and needs to be recomposed. In short, 'everything', 'total', 'totality' are words which have no need to be defined other than by what they are contrasted with. The word 'total' (or 'whole') functions both as a marker and as a sort of exclamatory shifter, which shunts all the words which it qualifies into the appropriate column: this is the case when the German professors say they would like to educate the 'whole' character of their students, when they declare that they prefer 'whole' insights to 'merely' analytic techniques or when they speak of the 'whole' nation.[45] In a given lexicon, in this case that of Jünger, these terms are associated with other *ideologically connected* words (*organische*,

Rangordnung, elementar, innen, and so many others). Thus each thought is presented as a constellation of words and themes which are linked by a purely sociological coherence, based on an intuitive sense of their politico-moral drift. This sense of the relations which obtain in practice between social positions and political attitudes, which is acquired from frequenting a field and which is a common factor relating even those who hold contradictory positions, is also what enables people to have an immediate 'sense' (and that in a quasi-explicit way at those moments of crisis when professional ideologies are forced to express themselves and when impressions of independence are weakened) of the ethical or political connotations of the apparently neutralized terms of specialized languages, to note for instance the conservative colouring of words as apparently anodyne as *Schauen* [intuitive insight], *Wesensschau* [perception of essences], *Erleben/Erlebnis* [personal experience] (the youth movements spoke frequently of *Bunderlebnis* [group experience], a sort of mystical *Mitsein* [communion]) or to perceive the hidden links between positivism or mechanization and egalitarianism or technology, or again, between utilitarianism and democracy.[46]

No single ideologue mobilizes all of the available schemata, which, for this reason, neither fulfil the same functions nor have equal importance in the different 'systems' in which they are inserted. Each thinker is thus able to produce, from the particular combination of the common schemata which he mobilizes, a discourse that is perfectly irreducible to the others, although it is only a transformed form of all the others. An ideology owes part of its impact to the fact that it is only ever activated in and through an orchestration of the various *habitus* which generate it: these systems of dispositions, which are singular, but which are objectively orchestrated, achieve their unity in and through the kaleidoscopic diversity of their products, which form a circle whose centre is both everywhere and nowhere.

The 'conservative revolutionaries',[47] whether they were

bourgeois who were excluded by the nobility from the prestigious posts of State administration, or petty bourgeois who were frustrated in the aspirations aroused by their educational success, found a magical solution to their contradictory expectations in the 'spiritual renaissance' and the 'German revolution'. 'The spiritual revolution' which was supposed to 'revitalize' the nation without revolutionizing its structure is what allowed these actual or potential *déclassés* to reconcile their desire to maintain a privileged position in the social order and to rebel against the order denying them this position, with their hostility to the bourgeoisie who excluded them and their repugnance for the socialist revolution that threatened all the values which helped to distinguish them from the proletariat. Their regressive yearning for a reassuring reintegration in the organic totality of an autarchic agrarian (or feudal) society is simply the counterpart of a hostile fear of anything in the present which announces a threat for the future, whether that threat is capitalist or marxist; they fear the capitalist materialism of the bourgeoisie as much as the godless rationalism of the socialists. But the 'conservative revolutionaries' give their movement its intellectual respectability by sometimes clothing their regressive ideas in the borrowed languages of marxism and progress, and by preaching chauvinism and reaction in the language of humanism. This cannot help but increase the structural ambiguity of their discourse and its seductive impact on even the university milieu.

> The ambiguity which characterizes the entire *völkisch* or 'conservative revolutionary' ideology is what enables thinkers like Lagarde, for instance, to seduce liberal academics who, like Ernst Troeltsch, acknowledge the great tradition of German idealism, with its aesthetic-cum-heroic vision of men and nations, its pseudo-religious faith in the irrational, the supernatural, and the divine, its glorification of 'Genius', its contempt for political and economic man, *for ordinary, everyday man*, along with the political culture which suits his desires, and its repugnance for modernity (cf. Stern, *Politics of Cultural*

Despair, especially pp. 82–94). The philosopher Franz Böhm sees in Lagarde the central defender of the Germanic spirit against Cartesian rationalism and optimism (cf. F. Böhm, *Anti-Cartesianismus, Deutsche Philosophie im Widerstand* (Leipzig, 1938), pp. 274ff., quoted by Stern, ibid., p. 93 and n.). In short, if, as Mosse remarks, the workers were ignorant of the conservative revolutionary message, the educated bourgeoisie was impregnated with it.[48] And the situation of crisis which affected academics must have helped weaken the resistance that normally accompanied their statutory contempt for fashionable essay writers.

Thus, although professional historians displayed some reservations over Spengler's methods, the most conservative among them at least were ready to welcome the vehemence of his conclusions. Knowing the in-built hostility academics feel for 'popularizers', we can imagine how strong their ideological sympathy must have been for Eduard Meyer, the most famous historian of antiquity of his times, to write: 'Spengler has brilliantly described precisely these elements of inner disintegration (*Zersetzung*) in the sections (of his *Decline of the West*) devoted to criticism of presently dominant points of view, in the chapters on the state and on politics, on democracy and parliamentary government with its ugly party machinations, on the all-powerful press, on the nature of the metropolis, on economic life, money, and machines.'[49] We know that among the most eminent academics Spengler enjoyed a reputation as a thinker which is still extant (as witness for example the laboured homage which, in his review of my study, *Die politische Ontologie Martin Heideggers*, Hans-Georg Gadamer pays to 'the extraordinary imagination and the powers of synthesis deployed by Spengler in his solitary research').[50] As for Heidegger, who picks up a number of Spengler's themes, but euphemizes them (the function of the dogs and the donkeys in Heraclitus' Fragment 97, which is explicated, among other fragments, in *An Introduction to Metaphysics* [(New Haven, Conn., Yale University Press, 1987), p. 132], devolves in Spengler to the lion and the cow), we know that he mentioned on several occasions the importance which he accorded to Jünger's thought. In an essay dedicated to Jünger, with whom he nourished a considerable acquaintance and correspondence, Heidegger writes: 'In the winter of 1939 to 1940, I explained *The Worker* in a small circle of university professors. They were astonished that such a clear-sighted book had been available for years and that none had yet learned by himself to dare make the attempt to let his glance move towards the optics of the *Worker* and to do some planetary thinking' (Heidegger, 'Concerning "The Line"', in *The Question of Being* (New York, Vision Press, 1959), p. 43).[51]

The structural ambiguity of a system of thought based on a dual refusal, whose logical outcome is the *self-destructive* notion of a 'conservative revolution', is written into the generative structure which sustains it, that is, the desperate effort to overcome a set of insuperable alternatives through a kind of headlong flight, whether heroic or mystical: it is no coincidence that the book where Möller van den Bruch, one of the prophets of 'revolutionary conservatism', preached the mystical reunion of the Germanic past and the ideal Germany of the future, together with the rejection of bourgeois society and economics and the return to corporatism, was first called the 'Third Way', and then *The Third Reich*. The strategy of the 'third way', which expresses in the ideological order the objective position the authors hold in the social structure, gives rise, even when applied to different fields, to homologous kinds of discourse. Spengler reveals this generative structure in all its clarity: enquiring into the nature of the technical, he contrasts two classes of explanation, the first comprising the 'idealists and the ideologues, retarded epigons of the classicism of the times of Goethe', who hold the technical to be 'inferior' to 'culture' and who treat art and literature as the ultimate value; the second comprising 'Materialism – in its essence an English product – which was the fashion among the half-educated during the latter half of the nineteenth century, and the philosophy of liberal journalism and radical mass-meetings, of Marxist and social-ethical writers who looked upon themselves as thinkers and seers'.[52] The field of specific contradictions in relation to which Spengler constituted his problematics of technology is quite homologous to the one which orientates his political options, that is, the contradiction between liberalism and socialism, which it 'overcomes' through a series of very Heideggerian paradoxes: 'Marxism', he says somewhere, 'is the capitalism of the workers'. Alternatively, in a strategy which he shares with Niekisch and a few others, he identifies the Prussian virtues of authoritarianism, obedience, and national solidarity with those required by socialism, or again, like Jünger, he argues that everyone – from the entrepreneur to the manual labourer – is a worker.

And it is also in terms of a third-way strategy, intended to bypass a contradictory couple, capitalism and socialism, that Sombart organizes his thought: marxist socialism is at once too revolutionary and too conservative in that it is opposed neither to the development of industry nor to the values of industrial society; in so far as it rejects the forms but not the essence of modern civilization it represents a degenerate species of socialism.[53] Such is the heart of this kind of misguided radicalism: combining the most violent hatred of industry and technology with the most intransigent elitism and the crudest contempt for the masses, he aims to substitute his 'true religion' for the theory of the class struggle, which by reducing man to the level of a swine [*Schweinehund*], endangers the souls of the masses and forms an obstacle to the development of a harmonious social life.[54] Niekisch, the principal representative of 'national Bolshevism', arrives at conclusions similar to those of Spengler, starting from virtually contradictory strategies, since he counts on nationalism, militarism, and the cult of heroism to draw the middle classes into the revolution. Identifying class with nation, Niekisch sees the German worker as a 'soldier of the State' who must show all of the great Prussian virtues, obedience, discipline, self-sacrifice, etc.

We find the pursuit of a very similar logic in *Der Arbeiter* by

Ernst Jünger, who, despite his links with Niekisch (as a contributor to his journal *Widerstand*), is the intellectual spokesman of the conservative revolutionaries, whose racist theories he promulgates.[55] He aims to overcome the antithesis between democracy and socialism, which was quintessentially formulated by Sombart: at one extreme we have liberal democracy, defined as individualism, as psychological and social anarchy, seen as the reign of the bourgeois 'who has no relation with the totality' and who chooses comfort and safety as his supreme values; and at the other extreme we have socialism, incapable of ushering in a new order, and judged to derive from the projection of bourgeois models onto the labour movement, that is the 'masses', the social form 'within which the individual is conceived'. This antagonism can only be overcome by the inauguration of a new order founded on 'planned labour', thanks to which the 'new breed of Worker' (*der Arbeiter*) controls technology through his superior technicism.

The 'new breed of Worker', overcoming both bourgeois and proletarian, 'in whom individual values, but also the values of the masses, will be overcome', as Rauschnigg was to say, has nothing in common with the real worker, depicted with all the colouring of class prejudice; his is the realm of 'organic construction' which has nothing in common with the 'mechanical masses'. It is more or less impossible to give an analytic account of this woolly mythology, which uses the perspectives of the 'conservative revolution' to map out its *conciliatio oppositorum*, which grants access to everything simultaneously, Prussian discipline and individual merit, authoritarianism and populism, the machine age and heroic chivalry, the division of labour and the organic totality. The Worker, in his role as modern hero, is confronted with the 'arena of work' where 'the demand for freedom arises in the guise of the demand for work' and where 'freedom has an existential quality', he is in close contact with the 'primitive' (in the sense of 'the elemental') and he is thereby able to gain access to a 'unitary life'; he is not corrupted by culture; he is placed in conditions of existence which, like those of the battlefield, call into question distinctions between the individual and the masses, as well as those of social 'rank'; he it is who mobilizes technology, which is in itself a neutral instrument. All this predisposes him to impose a new social order of a military nature, a sinister Prussian variant of the heroic technocracy dreamed up by Marinetti and the Italian Futurists: 'In the Prussian concept of duty we find a leaning towards the elementary, as witness the rhythm of military marches, the death penalty for heirs to the throne, the superb battles won thanks to the loyalty of the aristocracy and their well-trained soldiers. The only possible heir of the Prussian spirit is the Worker, who does not exclude the "elementary", but includes it; he has studied in the school of anarchy, learning how to break traditional bonds; thus he is forced to execute his will to freedom in a new era, in a new arena and through a new aristocracy'.[56] In short, the solution here consists in curing illness with illness, in seeking in technology and in that pure product of technology, the Worker made one with himself through the totalitarian State, the means to overcome technology.[57] 'On the one hand, the totally technical space will allow total domination, on the other hand, only such a domination will totally dispose of the technical'.[58] The solution to the antinomy is obtained by pushing it to an extreme: as in mystical thought, tension pushed to its extreme is resolved by a complete reversal of the thesis into the antithesis. It is the same magical logic of the marriage of opposites which leads this extremist fringe of the conservative revolutionaries to think up the concept of the Führer, which articulates an extreme case of the paradox that it is supposed to resolve, by fusing the cult of the hero with a mass movement. This calls to mind the poem by Stephan George (another of Heidegger's spiritual masters), *Algabal*: Algabal, the symbol of apocalyptic renewal, is a tender yet cruel nihilist leader who lives in artificial palaces and who, out of ennui, commits acts of great cruelty which he hopes will bring renewal through their cataclysmic impact.[59] Following a logical development analogous to this, Jünger's fantastical populism, a phantasmatic denial of marxism, reconciles the cult of the people (*Volk*) with an aristocratic hatred of the 'masses', transfigured by mobilization into an organic unity; he overcomes the horror of the anonymous monotony and empty uniformity which is written all over the workers' faces [60] by means of that perfect realization of empty uniformity, military mobilization: freeing the Worker from 'alienation' (as interpreted by the *Jugendbewegung*) means freeing him from freedom by alienating him into becoming subsumed into the person of the Führer. [61]

The clearest indication of what Heidegger means is his admission to Jünger that 'the "question about technology" owes enduring advancement to the descriptions in *The Worker*'. [62] Their ideological agreement on this topic is complete, as witness this extract from a speech given by Heidegger, during his period as Rector, on 22 January 1934: 'Knowledge and the possession of knowledge, as National Socialism understands these words, *does not divide into classes*, but binds and unites *Volksgenossen* and social and occupational groups (*Stände*) in the one great will of the State. Like these words "knowledge" and "*Wissenschaft*", "worker" and "work", too, have a *transformed meaning* and a *new sound*. The "worker" *is not, as Marxism claimed*, a mere object of exploitation. The workers (*Arbeiterstand*) are not the class of the disinherited (*Die Klasse der Enterbten*) who are rallying for the general class struggle.' [63] Beyond this almost literal coincidence with Heidegger of one of the central points of the 'political philosophy' developed in *Der Arbeiter*, it is the very heart of Heideggerian ontology, his vision of being and time, of freedom and nothingness, which finds at least implicit expression in the metaphysical-cum-political pathos of *Der Arbeiter*, that is in a form which allows us to glimpse its properly political foundation. Thus Heidegger retraces the self-same stages of the Jüngerian way when he affirms that it is in 'extreme danger' that we discover the fact that 'the coming to presence of technology harbours in itself what we least suspect, the possible upsurgence of saving power', or again, following the same logic, that it is the realization of the essence of metaphysics in the essence of technology, the ultimate accomplishment of the metaphysics of the will to power, which enables the overcoming of metaphysics.[64] The aim of Jüngerian nihilism, which sets itself up as a revolt against European decadence, is to substitute action for contemplation and give priority to the resoluteness of the act of choosing over the end chosen, and, ultimately, to prefer the will to will, in Heidegger's expression, to the will to power. Jünger's bellicose aestheticism is basically inspired by a hatred of weakness and irresoluteness, of the self-destructive uncertainty of reasonable reason, and also of the gap between words and sensory, sensual reality. And, although he articulates his antirationalist nihilism and the social forces which led to the rise of National Socialism in a cruder and more brutal, and therefore clearer, manner than the learned German professor of philosophy, he joins the author of *Being and Time* in this virtual preference for risk and danger, which incites people to take up an extreme position where they appreciate freedom in the moment of its destruction, and assume their responsibilities by experiencing the elementary violence of the here and now: 'Here anarchy is the touchstone of the indestructible, which feels pleasure in testing itself against annihilation'. It is in flirting with annihilation, as one plays with fire, that one tempers oneself and experiences one's freedom. Historical progress is no more than a sort of dynamic vacuum, absence in motion, a movement from nothing to nowhere; situated 'beyond value', it 'possesses no qualities'. There is a need to 'pass beyond the point where nothingness (*das Nichts*) seems more desirable than anything which harbours the slightest trace of doubt' and thus to join up with 'a more primitive community of souls, a primal race, which has not yet emerged as subject from its historic task and is therefore available for fresh vocations'.[65] Nationalism, with its apologia for the German race and its imperialist ambitions, can speak the political or semi-political language of resolution and mastery, of commandment and obedience, of willpower, death, and annihilation, in terms of a total mobilization; but it can also, as in Heidegger, speak the metaphysical or quasi-metaphysical language of the will to power as will to will, as affirmation of the will placed in the service not of any ends, but of self-overcoming, or again, the language of the resolute confrontation of death as authentic experience of freedom.

In Jünger, the phantasms and slogans of political nihilism lie close to the surface of the Nietszchean style; in Heidegger, political nihilism, and the Nietzschean tradition itself, not to mention the 'conservative revolutionary' vulgate of the Jüngers and the Spenglers, are subordinated to the ontological meditation of a reader of the pre-Socratics, Aristotle, and the Christian theologians, in such a way that the solitary search of the authentic thinker seems to have nothing in common with the opportunistic theorizing of the warrior bored with lesser combats. The frontier is the one that separates the layman from the professional, who knows the weight of words, because he is at least familiar in practice with the arena where his speech will have to fight for breathing space, that is, *the field of simultaneously possible stances* in relation to which his own position will be defined negatively and differentially. It is his knowledge of this space of possibilities which enables him to 'foresee objections', that is, to anticipate the significance and value which, depending on the prevailing taxonomies, will be attached to a given stance, and to undermine in advance any inadmissible interpretations. Here 'philosophical significance' and 'philosophical meaning' are identical to the practical or conscious mastery of the conventional signs which structure the philosophical space, enabling the professionals to *distance* themselves from positions already allocated, and to *disclaim* anything that is at all likely to be imputed to them ('Heidegger *disclaims* any pessimistic intention'), in short, to affirm *their difference* in and through a form endowed with every sign needed to make it a *recognized* form. A thought system socially recognized as philosophical is a thought system which implies reference to the field of philosophical stances and a reasonably conscious grasp of the implications of the position which it itself occupies in that field. Thus we may contrast the professional philosopher with the 'primitive philosopher' who, like the 'primitive painter' in the realm of art, does not truly understand what he is doing or saying. Because he is ignorant of the specific history of which the philosophical field is the result, and which is incorporated into socially instituted positions as well as built into its specific problematics in terms of a space of possible stances for the holders of different positions, the amateur delivers up crude thought, destined, as *The Worker* was for Heidegger, to become the raw material of the knowing meditations of the true professional, who is able to constitute as such the *problem* which the layman is tackling unwittingly. It may even happen that the latter is so completely ignorant of the basic rules of the game that he becomes an object of sport or mockery for professional thinkers. Thus when G. E. Moore becomes guilty of the kind of anachronism that consists in taking scepticism seriously and discussing this problem as if Kant (and the distinction between the transcendental and the empiric) had never existed, thereby suspending the kind of suspension of ordinary belief that defines strictly philosophical belief, he is exposed to the most terrible verdict that philosophers can deliver, however much they may preach the virtues of a calculated naïvety seeking to return to original values: 'Moore is naïve where Sextus is merely innocent'.[66] (This, we might note in passing, is the strategy that philosophers use spontaneously against any hostile questioning based on 'common sense', or against any scientific objectification of the presumptions inherent in belonging to a philosophical field, that is, the appropriate mental postures and attitudes entailed by this social space as it forms its strictly philosophical *illusio*.)

We might suppose that a philosopher as skilled in his profession as Heidegger knows what he is doing when he chooses Jünger as an object of reflection (especially collective and

public): Jünger asked the only (political) questions which
Heidegger agreed to answer, the only (political) questions
which he *made his own*, at the cost of a work of *retranslation*,
which enables us to study the mechanics of the philosophical
mode of thought. The transfer which he operates from one
mental (and social) space to another supposes a radical divide,
comparable to the one which, in another field, has been called
an 'epistemological divide', or 'break'. The frontier between
politics and philosophy is a genuine ontological threshold: the
notions relating to practical, everyday experience, and the
words that denote them (which are often the same), undergo a
radical transformation which renders them barely recognizable in the eyes of those who have agreed to make the magical
leap into the other universe. Thus Jean-Michel Palmier no
doubt expresses the common opinion of commentators when
he writes: 'It is difficult not to be surprised by the importance
Heidegger attributed to this book (*The Worker*)'.[67] Philosophical alchemy (like mathematical alchemy when it transforms a speed into a derivative or an area into an integer, or
judicial alchemy when it transmutes a quarrel or a conflict into
a trial) is a *metabasis eis allo genos*, what Pascal would have
called a passage into another order, which is inseparable from
a *metanoia*, a change of social space which supposes a change
of mental space.

Thus we are able to explain why the philosopher, whose
profession it is to ask questions, especially those questions
which the received wisdom of the everyday world makes it
impossible, by definition, to ask, never replies to 'naïve' questions, that is, questions which are irrelevant or impertinent
in his eyes, for instance those common-sense queries which
people may have about his philosophical questions (on the
existence of the external world, on the existence of others,
etc.), and especially those questions which sociologists would
like to extrapolate from their own mental and social space in
order to apply them to the philosopher, such as questions we
would term 'political', that is, *openly*, therefore naïvely,

political. But the philosopher can only reply to philosophical questions, that is to questions which are put to him, or which he asks himself, in the only language which he finds pertinent, philosophical language, and which he is only able to answer (in practice as well as in theory) when he has retranslated them into his philosophical idiolect. Yet one should not make the mistake of interpreting this commentary as an aphoristic attack mounted by a hostile moralist. The distance kept by the philosopher is merely the position most usually adopted as the obvious solution for anyone who wishes to enter any learned milieu, that is, to be recognized as a legitimate participant and, *a fortiori*, to succeed in it; this position seems self-evident to anyone who is equipped with the appropriate *habitus*, that is, who is adjusted in advance to the structural necessity of the field and ready to accept the presumptions objectively implied by the fundamental rules of the field, often without being aware of them.

In short, we should not expect the philosopher to express himself in the raw, using the crude language of politics, and we should read between the lines of Heidegger's commentary on Jünger's text: '*The Worker* belongs in the phase of "active nihilism" (Nietzsche). The action of the work consisted – and in a changed function still consists – in the fact that it makes the "total work character" of all reality visible, from the figure of the worker'. And, two pages later: 'However, the optics and the horizon which guide the describing are no longer or not yet correspondingly determined as they were formerly. For now you no longer take part in the action of active nihilism, which is also already thought of in *The Worker* in Nietzsche's sense in the direction towards an overcoming. No longer taking part, however, by no means already means standing outside of nihilism, especially not when the essence of nihilism is not nihilistic and the history of this essence is older and yet remains younger than the historically determinable phases of the various forms of nihilism'. What is being suggested through all these overtones, is that the problem of totalitarianism, of the totalitarian State, which manages to use technology as an intermediary to impose its domination on the whole of existence, is still open to question, even when that particular form of nihilism has historically come to an end. We can follow the rest of the argument more easily: 'No one with any insight will still deny today that nihilism is in the most varied and most hidden forms of "the normal state" of man. . . . The best evidences of this are the exclusively re-active attacks against nihilism, which, instead of entering into a discussion with its essence, strive for the restoration of what has been. They seek salvation in flight, namely in flight from a glimpse of the worthiness of questioning the metaphysical position of man. The same flight is also urgent where apparently all metaphysics is abandoned and is replaced by logistics, sociology, and psychology'.[68] Here too we may read that the totalitarian State and modern science constitute the 'necessary consequences of the essential deployment of the technical', and that – although here his paradox is strained to breaking point – the only truly non-reactionary thought is that which confronts Nazism in order to 'resolutely' contemplate its essence instead of fleeing from it. This was also the sense of the famous phrase in *An Introduction to Metaphysics*, a lecture course given in 1935 and published unmodified in 1953, on the 'inner truth and greatness' of National Socialism, 'namely the encounter between global technology and modern man'.[69] There is a clear line running from the repressed aristocratism of *Sein und Zeit* to the philosophical assimilation of Nazism, which becomes as it were banalized in terms of a paroxysmic manifestation of one stage in the development of the essence of technology. Jünger is well placed to read between the lines of this virtually unrepentant revaluation of a trajectory which he largely shares with Heidegger, even including his inability to assume resolute responsibility for the consequences of the appeal to responsibility.[70] Nazi nihilism, being a heroic attempt to overcome limits, in Jüngerian fashion, and overcome the very nihilism of which it is the extreme form, constitutes the ultimate affirmation of ontological difference: all that is left is to resolve to confront this separation, this insuperable dualism which lies between Being itself and the actual entities from which it is for ever separated. The heroic philosophy of despising death, instead of running off to seek assistance, must give way to an equally heroic philosophy, the resolute confrontation of this absolute schism. The refusal of all metaphysical transcendence, which is the supreme stage of the will to will and a final effort to ignore the absence of Being (which Heidegger detects and condemns in the last writings of Jünger, especially 'Concerning "The Line" '), leads to a mystical *Gelassenheit*, in anticipation of an anti-nihilist revelation of Being.

Ultimately, when the third way (in Möller van den Bruck's sense) of heroic overcoming is definitively closed, we discover the desperate powerlessness which forms its motivation (the powerlessness of the intellectual, placed in the position of dominated–dominator in the social structure). When powerful thought, and active encouragement of the active nihilism of total mobilization as spiritual purification, have come to an end, there remains the philosophy of powerlessness, the *passive nihilism* which maintains just as radical a difference between the thinker who has attained detachment, and all those, whether powerful or not, who yield to the oblivion of Being.

2

The philosophical field and the space of possibilities

But Heidegger is not addressing Jünger alone. His discourse is defined, subjectively and objectively, in relation to two different social and mental spaces, the space of political essay writing and the philosophical space properly speaking. Even in a speech on technology which is dedicated to Jünger, who is thus the ostensible addressee, he is in a way aiming 'over his head' at quite a different audience (as witness the title which he was to give, on its publication, to this apparently public text on technology: 'The Question of Being'). As a philosophically subversive thinker, Heidegger knows and acknowledges the legitimate stakes of the philosophical field well enough (his explicit references to the canonical authors, past or present, are sufficient evidence of this), and he respects the absolute rift that academic ethics have driven between culture and politics[1] profoundly enough to submit his social phantasms and his ethical or political dispositions, without consciously intending to do so, to a restructuring liable to render them *misrecognizable*.[2]

Whereas he is a contemporary of Spengler and Jünger in the public time of politics, Heidegger is the contemporary of Cassirer and Husserl in the autonomous history of the philosophical field. If, as we have just seen, he *is situated* in a given moment of the political history of Germany, he *situates himself* at a stage in the internal history of philosophy, or, more precisely, in the series of successive returns to Kant (which are different each time, because each one is elaborated against the background of the preceding one), which punctuate the history of German academic philosophy: as Cohen and the Marburg school reject the Fichtean reading of Kant, Heidegger denounces the reading of the great neo-Kantians, who, according to him, reduce the *Critique of Pure Reason* to a search for the conditions of the possibility of science, making reflection a slave to truths which precede it in theory as well as in practice.[3] One can also, using other genealogies, situate him at the crossroads of traditions founded by Kierkegaard, Husserl, and Dilthey. Situating him in this field implies situating him in the history of the field, that is, integrating the historical process of the field into his work, by recognizing and understanding the historically constituted problematic which is founded in its practice. The philosophical genealogy that the philosopher claims for himself in his retrospective interpretations is a well-founded fiction. The inheritor of a learned tradition always refers to his predecessors or his contemporaries in the very distance which he adopts towards them. It would therefore be perfectly vain to try to understand separately from its relations with the philosophical field in which it is rooted, a philosophical thought as manifestly professorial as that of Heidegger: who never ceased to think – and to think of himself – in relation to other thinkers – and increasingly so, in an apparent paradox, as his autonomy and originality became clearer. All of Heidegger's fundamental options, those whose source lies in the deepest dispositions of his *habitus* and their expression in the 'primordial' pairs of antagonistic concepts borrowed from the spirit of the age, are defined with reference to an already constituted philosophical space, that is, in relation to a field of philosophical stances which reproduces in its own logical terms the network of social positions extant in the philosophical field. It is by means of this permanent reference to the field of possible philosophical stances that the philosophical transposition of politico-moral stances is effected; this process dictates not only the problems, but also *the structured universe of possible solutions* which determines in advance the philosophical meaning of any stance, however original (as for instance an anti-Kantian, or a neo-Thomist one). It is this reference which, by means of the (more or less consciously felt) homology between the structure of the philosophical stances and the structure of overtly political stances, demarcates the very restricted range of philosophical stances compatible with the politico-moral options of any given thinker.

Such stances claim, and are considered, to be philosophical in so far, and only in so far, as they are defined in relation to the field of stances philosophically known and recognized at a given moment in time; in so far as they succeed in being acknowledged as pertinent responses to the *problematic* which is most pressing at any given moment, in terms of the antagonisms which constitute the field. The relative autonomy of the field is shown in its capacity to insert a system of legitimate problems and topics for study among the politico-moral dispositions which both launch the discourse and shape its final form, and thereby to subject any expressive drive to a systematic transformation. Imposing philosophical form entails observing political formalities, and the *transformation* implied by a transfer from one social space (which is inseparable from a mental space) to another, tends to disguise the relation between the final product and the social determinants which lie behind it, since a philosophical stance is no more than the homologue, in a different system, of a 'naïve' politico-moral stance.

The dual allegiance of the philosopher, defined by the position which is assigned to him in social space (and, more precisely, in the structure of the field of power) and by the position which he holds in the field of philosophical production, is what fuels the transformation processes which belong as much to the unconsciously functioning operations of the field, retranslated in terms of a *habitus*, as they do to conscious strategies of systematization. Thus the relation which Heidegger maintains with the most striking positions of the political space, liberalism and socialism, marxism or 'conservative-revolutionary' thought, or with the corresponding social positions, are only constituted in practice through a whole series of relations homologous to the fundamental opposition which is at once displayed and transfigured there. It is above all the relation of dual refusal and dual distancing which is entailed by belonging to an intellectual aristocracy, whose elitism, on the one hand, is threatened by the mortal danger of *Vermassung*, the 'levelling down' and 'lowering of standards' to which an influx of students and junior teachers exposes it, and, on the other hand, whose moral authority as counsellor of princes or pastor to the masses is threatened by the arrival of an industrial bourgeoisie and of popular movements able to define their own objectives. This is a relation which is reproduced, in a specific form, in the relation of philosophy to the other disciplines. The body of professional thinkers, whose claims have been threatened since the end of the nineteenth century by the growing ability of the natural sciences to reflect upon their own processes, and by the emergence of social sciences aiming to appropriate the traditional objects of philosophical reflection, remains in a state of permanent alert against psychologism and, especially, positivism, which claims to confine philosophy within the limits of an epistemology (*Wissenschaftstheorie*) (the adjectives *naturwissenschaftlich* and *positivistisch* function as irrevocable condemnations, even among historians).[4] In the eyes of a generally very conservative academic world, which was dominated by the 'German nationalists',[5] sociology, which was seen as a French, and a plebeian, science, and which was categorized as a kind of critical extremism (with Mannheim in particular), combining all evils: the prophets of *Verstehen* are full of contempt for this reductionist, populist enterprise even when they do not mention it explicitly, and especially when it takes the form of a philosophy of knowledge.[6] And this relation between philosophy and science may be seen more specifically in the relations that Heidegger entertained with the neo-Kantians, among whom his contemporaries distinguished the so-called South-Western tradition, with Windelband and then Rickert (Heidegger's thesis supervisor), and the Marburg school, whose principal representative was Herman Cohen, a favourite butt of the ideologues of the Third Reich.[7] Windelband, a professor at Heidelberg, later succeeded by Husserl, proffered a critique of Cohen's leanings towards agnostic positivism which prefigures Heidegger's arguments against the Kantian critique of metaphysics. The empiricist epistemology which the Marburg school discovers in the work of Kant tends to replace philosophical criticism by a causal and psychological analysis of experience, inclining on the one hand towards Hume and on the other towards Comte, and thus tending to dissolve philosophy in epistemology.[8] The more metaphysically inspired Kantianism is also represented by Alois Riegl, who was drawn towards *Naturphilosophie*, and by Heidegger's other master, Lask, who, as Gurvitch says, transforms transcendental analysis into ontological metaphysics.[9] At the other extreme, Cohen and Cassirer stand out as the prestigious heirs of the great liberal tradition and of European Enlightenment humanism. Cassirer tries to show 'that the idea of the republican constitution as such is by no means a foreign intruder within the German intellectual tradition', but, on the contrary, the culmination of Idealist philosophy.[10] As for Cohen, he offers a socialist interpretation of Kant, whereby the categorical imperative, which orders us to treat other people as ends and not means, is treated as the moral programme of the future ('The idea of the pre-eminence of Humanity as an end becomes by this means alone the Idea of socialism, so that each man may be defined as a Final end in himself').[11]

Because of the dominant position held by the various representatives of neo-Kantianism, the holders of the other important positions need to be defined in relation to them (or more precisely, in opposition to them), as well as in opposition to the various psychologies of empirical consciousness – psychologism, vitalism, or empirico-criticism – which some of them seemed to encourage with their more or less distorted transcendental analysis. This applies to Husserlian phenomenology, internally divided between an ontology and a transcendental, anti-psychologist logic. It also affects the whole more or less direct inheritance of *Lebensphilosophie*, henceforth orientated towards the philosophy of civilization: comprising, in its academic variant, the heirs of Dilthey (whose influence on Heidegger is well known), and also, to a certain extent, those of Hegel, Lipps, Litt, or Spranger; and, in its popularized version, systems of thought like that of Ludwig Klages, influenced by Bergson and very close to neo-conservative literature (with, for instance, its exaltation of *Einfühlung*, empathy, and *Anschauung*, intuition, and its reliance on simplistic alternatives, like soul and intellect, to found a passionate critique of the intellectualization of the world and its domination by technology). There is also the logical positivism of the Wittgensteins and Carnaps and Poppers: in a manifesto published in 1929 the Vienna Circle attacked the semantic confusion rampant in academic philosophy and declared its sympathy for progressive movements, suspecting that 'those who hold on to the past in the social field also cultivate [outdated] positions in metaphysics and theology'.[12]

Such was the space of philosophical possibilities, at the moment when Heidegger passed his *Abitur* [school leaving certificate] at Constance, and made his début in a philosophical field whose lower depths were haunted by two great repressed figures, namely marxism, and the reactionary metaphysics of the 'conservative revolutionaries'. Belonging to the philosophical field in that place and at that time meant being faced with the problem or the programme whose oppositions formed its structure: the problem of how to overcome the philosophy of transcendental consciousness without falling back into realism or the psychologism of the empirical subject, or, worse, into some form or other of 'historicist' reduction. What is extraordinary in Heidegger's philosophical enterprise is the fact that he intended to mount a revolutionary philosophical coup in *creating*, at the heart of the philosophical field, a new position, in relation to which all the other positions would have to be redefined: this position, which might have been inferred from certain efforts to overcome Kantianism, but which was missing from all the legitimate (that is, academically institutionalized) philosophical problematics, was in a way called for by certain political or literary movements outside the field like the *George-Kreis* [Stephan George's Circle], and drafted into the field as an answer to the expectations of certain students or young assistant professors. In order to achieve such an upset of power relations at the heart of the philosophical field, and give a form of respectability to stances that were heretical, and thus likely to appear vulgar, Heidegger had to combine the 'revolutionary' dispositions of a rebel with the specific authority granted by the accumulation of a considerable capital within the field itself. Heidegger had been Husserl's assistant professor (since 1916), had become professor ordinarius at Marburg (in 1923), and thus radiated the glamour of an avant-garde thinker able to exploit a critical conjuncture both inside and outside the university in order to impose a language at once revolutionary and conservative: prophets, as Weber observed in the case of ancient Judaism and of heresiarchs in general, are often defectors from the priestly caste who invest a considerable specific capital in subversion of the priestly order and who forge from a renewed reading of the most sacred authorities the weapons of a revolution designed to restore tradition to its original, authentic form.

The *habitus* of this 'professor ordinarius', whose origins were in the lesser rural petty bourgeoisie, and who was unable to think and speak politics without using mental and verbal patterns borrowed from ontology – to such an extent that the Nazi Rector's address became a metaphysical profession of faith – is in practice the enabling factor establishing homology between the philosophical and political fields: in fact it absorbs the whole set of dispositions and interests associated with the different positions held in the different fields (in the social space, it is that of the *Mittelstand* and the academic fraction of that class; in the structure of the academic field, it is that of philosophy, etc.), as well as those associated with the social *trajectory* leading to these positions, that of the first-generation university teacher who, despite his success, is placed in a false position in the intellectual field. It is a *habitus* which, being an integrated product of relatively independent factors, is able to integrate such determinisms permanently (despite their origins in different orders) into practices and products which are essentially *overdetermined* (we might think, for instance, of these thinkers' concern for the question of roots, of origins).

It seems likely that Heidegger's social trajectory helps to explain his absolutely exceptional polyphonic talent, his gift for making connections between problems which previously existed only in fragmentary form, scattered around the political and philosophical fields, while yet giving the impression that he was posing them in a more 'radical' and more 'profound' manner than anyone before him. His rising trajectory, leading across different social universes, predisposed him better than a plane trajectory to speak and think in several spaces at once, to address audiences other than his peers (like those more or less fantasized 'peasants' who exist primarily as a foil for Heidegger's rejection of the rootless intellectual); and his belated and purely scholastic acquisition of an educated language may well have fostered that relation to language which enabled him to play on the learned harmonics of ordinary language at the same time as reviving the ordinary harmonics of learned language (which is one of the causes of the powerful effect of prophetic estrangement which *Sein und Zeit* produces).[13] But above all we cannot understand the extraordinary position of Martin Heidegger in the philosophical field without taking into account his awkward, strained relation to the intellectual world, which he owed to an improbable, and thereby all the more exceptional social trajectory. There is no doubt in fact that Heidegger's hostility to the grand masters of Kantianism, especially Cassirer, was rooted in a profound incompatibility with their alien *habitus*: 'On the one hand, you had this dark, athletic little man, an accomplished skier, with energetic but impassive features, a hard, diffi-cult man, totally committed to setting and solving problems with the deepest moral seriousness; and, on the other hand, a white-haired man, Olympian not only in appearance but also in spirit, with his open mind and his wide-ranging discussions, his relaxed features and his indulgent amiability, his vitality and adaptability, and, finally, his aristocratic distinction'.[14] We can quote the words of Cassirer's wife herself: 'We had been explicitly warned about Heidegger's odd appearance; we knew about his rejection of all social conventions and also his hostility towards neo-Kantians, especially Cohen. His penchant for anti-semitism was not unfamiliar to us, either. . . .'[15] All the guests had arrived, the women in evening gowns, the men in dinner suits. At a point when the dinner had been interrupted for some time with seemingly endless speeches, the door opened, and an inconspicuous little man came into the room, looking as awkward as a peasant who had stumbled into a royal court. He had black hair and dark piercing eyes, rather like some workman from southern Italy or Bavaria; an impression which was soon confirmed by his regional accent. He was wearing an old-fashioned black suit'. And she goes on to say: 'For me, what seemed the most worrying thing, was his deadly seriousness and his total lack of a sense of humour'.[16]

Of course we must not allow ourselves to be taken in by appearances: the 'existential suit'[17] and the local accent seem somewhat ostentatious in the case of a 'brilliant' university teacher, who was already basking in the admiration of his masters and his pupils.[18] Like his idealistic references to the peasant world, they sound like a pose, and could well be no more than a way of converting his awkward relation to the intellectual world into a philosophical attitude. As a 'brilliant' intruder, an exclusive alien, Heidegger imported into the intellectual world another way of living the intellectual life, more 'serious' and more 'workmanlike' (for instance in his relation to philosophical texts and to language), but also more *absolute*: that of the *intellectual master* who claims a wider and more thoroughgoing remit than the defenders of a philosophy reduced to a reflection on knowledge and who, in exchange, feels that he owes it to his pastoral vocation and his role of moral conscience of the city to adopt an absolute and intransigent commitment in his whole exemplary existence.

The dual rejection entailed by the aristocratic populism of Heidegger is probably not unrelated to the more or less scandalized representation that he might have had, as a first-generation intellectual, of what seemed to him to be a paradoxical inversion, that is the 'democratic', 'republican', or even 'socialist' dispositions of those who, for him, formed the upper bourgeoisie, and from whom he felt separated in every respect, and especially as regards the 'authenticity' and sincerity of his populist convictions. It is easy enough to detect his viscerally antagonistic reactions to this verbose, frivolous humanism, in the series of oppositions which lie at the heart of his elaborate system, setting taciturn silence (*Verschwiegenheit*), the perfect expression of authenticity, against verbosity (*Gerede, Geschwätz*), rootedness (*Bodenständigkeit*), the core of the ideology of 'earth' and 'roots', against curiosity (*Neugier*), assimilated, no doubt by way of a mediatory Platonic topos, to the shifting nature of the emancipated mind and the rootlessness of the errant intellectual, associated through this key word with the figure of the Wandering Jew;[19] or, finally, the oversophisticated refinement of urban, Jewish 'modernity' against the archaic, rural, pre-industrial simplicity of the peasant who is as alien to the urban worker, the archetypal 'they' [*das Man*], as the errant intellectual, with neither roots nor bonds, faith nor allegiance, is to the 'pastor of Being'.[20]

His moral indignation and his revolt against the proprieties normally observed by intellectuals and students, are sometimes overtly revealed in certain statements or eye-witness accounts: 'he detested any "philosophy of civilization", as he did philosophical conferences; he seethed with emotional fury at the quantity of reviews that were founded after the First World War. He wrote with asperity to Scheler that his studies merely "updated" E. Von Hartmann, while other scholars, long after publishing a *Logos*, were publishing their *Ethos* and their *Kairos*. "What will be next week's joke? I think that the inside of a lunatic asylum would present a neater and more coherent picture than our century"' (K. Löwith, 'Les implications politiques de la philosophie de l'existence chez Heidegger', *Les Temps modernes*, 2 (1946), p. 346). And there is a whole representation of the 'careless' and facile life of (bourgeois?) students hidden between the lines of the Nazi Rector's address: 'The much celebrated "academic freedom" is being banished from the German University; for this freedom was not genuine, since it was only negative. It meant primarily *freedom from concern*, arbitrariness of intentions and inclinations, *lack of restraint* in what was done and left undone. The concept of the freedom of the German student is now brought back to its truth' (Heidegger, 'The Self-Assertion of the German University', *Review of Metaphysics*, no. 38 (March 1985), pp. 475–6). We know from other records (cf. Hühnerfeld, *In Sachen Heidegger*, p. 51) that Heidegger had little esteem for his colleagues, and that he did not want to be involved in academic philosophy, which he thought 'moribund'.

And we should doubtless see in his exalted encounter with an idealized peasant world rather a displaced and sublimated expression of his ambivalence towards the intellectual world, than an actual cause of this experience. Let it suffice to quote some significant moments of the radio broadcast where Heidegger explained his rejection of the chair in philosophy at Berlin, 'Why do we prefer to stay in the provinces?': 'When, in the darkness of a winter night, a snow storm surrounds the shelter (*die Hütte*) and covers everything, then the great moment of philosophy has arrived. Its questions must become simple and essential (*einfach und wesentlich*). . . . Philosophical labour should not be exercised as the isolated enterprise of an eccentric individual. It is absolutely central to the work of the peasant. . . . The town-dweller believes that he is "mingling with the people" when he deigns to have a long conversation with a peasant. When in the evening I interrupt my work and sit down on a bench by the fire or in the inglenook (*Herrgottswinkel*), then we often don't speak at all. We fall silent and smoke our pipes. . . . The intimate rapport of my work with the Black Forest and its inhabitants is based on a priceless, age-old rootedness (*Bodenständigkeit*) in the Alemanian-Swabian territory' (Heidegger, 'Warum Bleiben wir in der Provinz?', *Der Alemanne* (March 1934), quoted in Schneeberger, *Nachlese zu Heidegger* pp. 216–18). And later in the same speech Heidegger tells how, when he had received a second offer of appointment to Berlin, he went to see 'his old friend, a seventy-five year old peasant', who, without saying a word, indicated that he should refuse. An anecdote which is certain to find its place alongside Heraclitus' stove in philosophical hagiography.

Historians of philosophy too often forget that the great philosophical options which mark out the space of philosophical possibilities, such as neo-Kantianism, neo-Thomism, and phenomenology, are embodied in the palpable forms of people, who are themselves perceived in terms of their life-style, behaviour, and speech, their white hair and their Olympian looks, and that these philosophical options are associated with moral tendencies and political choices, which give them a concrete physiognomy. It is in relation to these palpable configurations, eclectically perceived, in sympathy or antipathy, indignation or complicity, that positions are experienced and stances defined: the simultaneously ethical, political, and philosophical 'sense of the game' which any successful investments and displacements in the philosophical field are bound to suppose, uses these overdetermined markers to chart its philosophical itinerary, which in practice merges the 'conservative revolution' with the counter-revolutionary overthrow of neo-Kantian critiques of metaphysics and the 'reign of reason'.

Heidegger applies his relatively rare specific competence, acquired first from his Jesuit school, then from the theologians of Freiburg, and later from reading the philosophical texts which he had to teach, to what he envisages as a *radical* enterprise of critical questioning (the adjective keeps recurring in his writings and correspondence), but also an academically respectable one. This apparently contradictory ambition leads him to make a symbolic union of two polar opposites. Thus his idea of a godless theology informing an initiatory academy, is an attempt to reconcile the esoteric elitism of small circles like the *George-Kreis*, from which he borrows his models of intellectual achievement (such as Hölderlin, rediscovered by Norbert von Hellingrath, or Reinhardt's *Parmenides*), with the ecological mystique of the *Jugendbewegung* or of Steiner's anthroposophy, which preach a return to rural simplicity and sobriety, forest walks, natural food, and hand-woven garments. The repetitive Wagnerian afflatus of Heidegger's style, which is so far removed (except perhaps in its intentions) from Stephan George's superbly anti-Wagnerian rhythmical and metrical play; his brand of avant-gardism which consists in 'defamiliarizing' the canonical authors;[21] his return to 'the world of necessitous actions', 'the familiar', and everyday existence;[22] his provincial asceticism as champion of natural products and regional dress, which seems like a petty-bourgeois caricature of the aesthetic asceticism of the great initiates, with their love for Italian wine and Mediterranean landscapes, Mallarméan and pre-Raphaelite poetry, classical clothing, and Dantesque profiles – everything, in this professorial, that is 'democratized' version of elitism betrays a man excluded from the aristocratic elite but unable to suppress his own aristocratic elitism.

In order to see how the exceptionally improbable stylistic amalgam produced by Heidegger is rigorously homologous with the ideological amalgam that it has to convey, we have only to restore Heidegger's language to the space of contemporary languages where its distinction and its social value are objectively defined: that is, to mention only the pertinent points: the conventional and hieratic language of Stephan George's type of post-Mallarméan poetry, the academic and rationalistic language of Cassirer's brand of neo-Kantianism, and finally the language of the 'theoreticians' of the 'conservative revolution' like Möller van den Bruck[23] or, closer to Heidegger in political terms, Ernst Jünger.[24] Unlike the language of post-symbolist poetry, which is strictly ritualized and highly purified, especially in its vocabulary, Heidegger's language, despite being its transposition onto the philosophical plane, exploits the licence implicit in the properly conceptual logic of *Begriffsdichtung*, to welcome words and themes (like *Fürsorge*, for instance) which are excluded not only from the esoteric discourse of the great initiates,[25] but also from the highly neutralized language of academic philosophy. Basing his authority on the philosophical tradition which invites one to exploit the infinite potential of thought which is contained in everyday language and popular proverbs,[26] Heidegger introduces into academic philosophy (along the lines suggested by the parable of Heraclitus' stove, which he glosses indulgently) words and things which had

previously been banished. Heidegger is close to the spokesmen of the 'conservative revolution', many of whose words
and theses he consecrates philosophically, but he distances
himself from it by imposing a form which sublimates the
'crudest' borrowings by inserting them in the network of
phonetic and semantic resonance which characterizes the
Hölderlin-style *Begriffsdichtung* of the academic prophet.
All of which situates him at the antipodes of the classical
academic style, with its several varieties of frigid rigour,
whether elegant and transparent in Cassirer, or tortured and
obscure in Husserl.

3

A 'conservative revolution' in philosophy

As a conservative revolutionary in philosophy, Heidegger presents the analyst with an almost insuperable problem. If we wish to analyse the specific nature of this revolution, and avoid accusations of 'naïvety', we must inevitably play the philosophers' game (which in one sense is only too easy, since there is so much to gain in exploiting the subjective and objective profits of the *illusio*) and accept all the assumptions that are inherent in the philosophical field and its history, and are therefore central to a subversive ambition, which can only sustain its philosophical revolution if it avoids calling such assumptions into question.[1] But if we wish to delineate this revolution and the social conditions of its appearance, we must categorically renounce all received opinion, whether it is the official philosophical doxa or the bias endemic to the 'naïve' insider, and we thus lay ourselves open to being judged ignorant of the game, that is to say, indifferent and incompetent, and risk leaving the faithful unmoved, by further reinforcing the image that the pure text intends to give of itself as a sacred, untouchable reality, allowing no scope for 'reduction'.[2]

While we can never be sure that we will ultimately overcome the inevitable ambiguity of an analysis constantly threatened by the temptations of indulgence or incomprehension, our ambition is to describe the properly social dimension of strategies whose philosophical and social aspects are inextricably mingled, since they are engendered in the social microcosm of the philosophical field. Thus we presume in fact (a presumption explicitly announced becomes a methodological postulate) that strictly philosophical interest is determined, as much in its very existence *qua* specific *libido sciendi* as in its orientations and applications, by the position held in the structure of the philosophical field at the moment in question, and is thereby determined by the field's whole history, which, in certain conditions, may be the source of a genuine overcoming of the limits ascribed to historicity.[3]

There is no doubt that it is in the philosophical field that Heidegger – and this is what makes him a philosopher – has primarily, if not exclusively, staked his credit, and that his prime objective is the creation of a new philosophical position, defined, fundamentally, in its relation to Kant or more exactly the neo-Kantians: the latter dominate the field under the aegis of a symbolic capital which serves as a guarantee for orthodox philosophical enterprises, namely, Kant's writings and the Kantian problematic. It is through this problematic, which in the social space takes the concrete form of neo-Kantian polemics over the legitimate questions of the moment, such as the problem of knowledge and the problem of values,[4] that the field and those who dominate it offer targets – and also limits – to the subversive ambitions of the newcomer. Heidegger is vastly learned, both in matters orthodox (having written several reviews of books on Kant, discussing in particular his relation to Aristotle) and in matters heterodox or even mildly heretical, as we can see from his doctoral thesis on Duns Scotus; and he approaches these problems with what we might call, by analogy with politics, a *theoretical line*. Since it is rooted in the depths of the *habitus*, this line does not originate in the logic of the philosophical field alone, and, furthermore, it serves in its turn to motivate choices made in the whole set of fields. We need to bear in mind the homologies which are established between the political field, the academic field, and the philosophical field, and in particular between the major oppositions which structure them, like the political opposition between liberalism and marxism, the academic opposition between the traditional humanities (including philosophy itself) and the natural sciences with their positivist dependencies, or the social sciences with their trappings of 'psychologism', 'historicism', and 'sociologism', and finally the philosophical apposition between the different forms of Kantianism, separated by divisions which, however 'pure' they may be, are not without resonance in the domains of politics or academic politics. Then we realize how *overdetermined*, both politically and academically, are the options selected as philosophically significant for the chosen theoretical line, on the strictly philosophical plane (which is doubtless supposed to be untainted by any political or academic considerations). There is no philosophical option – neither one that promotes intuition, for instance, nor, at the other extreme, one that favours judgement or concepts, nor yet one that gives precedence to the Transcendental Aesthetic over the Transcendental Analytic, or poetry over discursive language – which does not entail its concomitant academic and political options, and which does not owe to these secondary, more or less unconsciously assumed options, some of its deepest determinations.

What gives Heidegger's thought its exceptionally polyphonic and polysemic character, is no doubt its talent for speaking harmoniously in several registers at once, alluding (negatively) to socialism, science or positivism, through a purely philosophical reading of certain purely philosophical readings of the work of Kant (although these themselves have political implications). In whatever field, any determination is also a negation, and one cannot set up a theoretical line (any more than a political line or an artistic style, incidentally) without setting it up in opposition to other, rival lines, thus defining it in terms of a negation. Because the two terms of the various structurally homologous alternatives are rejected as a result of the same principles, the options (always of the third way) which are selected in the different mental (and social) spaces are immediately consonant, since they are structurally equivalent.

In confronting the neo-Kantian problematic, as much in the form where it is most alien, even most distasteful, to his politico-moral dispositions (in Cohen's works) as in the form (in the work of his privileged rival, Husserl) where it is most elaborately reworked and renewed, Heidegger gives the impression, because of the homology between the two spaces, that he is posing at the deepest, most radical level, some of the problems which are posed in the academic field (the question of the respective statuses of science and philosophy) and in the political field (the questions raised by the critical events of 1919). By refusing, as he does in *Kant and the Problem of Metaphysics*, to adopt the approach which consists in debating what legal definition should regulate the conduct of a science claiming factual status, he overturns the subordinate relation of philosophy to science which neo-Kantianism (similar in this to positivism) tends to establish at the risk of reducing philosophy to a simple reflection on science. By establishing philosophy as a fundamental science, which is able to found others, but cannot itself be founded, he restores to philosophy the autonomy which the school of Marburg had caused it to lose, and, by the same token, he turns the ontological question of the meaning of Being into the precondition of any enquiry into the validity of the positive sciences.[5]

This revolutionary reversal, a typical example of what one might call, with all due respect, the strategy of *Wesentlichkeit*, leads to another. Without following it right through to its logical conclusion, that is, absolute idealism, Cohen's approach leads him to give precedence to the problem of judgement over the problem of transcendental imagination. Cohen reduces intuition to the concept and aesthetics to logic, and, bracketing out the notion of the thing in itself, tends to substitute for the successful synthesis of Reason (posited by Hegel's panlogism) the incomplete synthesis of Understanding. Taking up and using against him the finitude that can be glimpsed through Cohen's affirmation of the imperfection of knowledge, Heidegger re-establishes the privilege of intuition and Aesthetics, making existential temporality the transcendental foundation of pure, but sensory Reason.

A philosophical strategy is at one and the same time a political strategy at the heart of the philosophical field: in revealing the metaphysics which underpins the Kantian critique of all metaphysics, Heidegger appropriates for 'foundational thinking' (*das wesentliche Denken*) – which treats Reason, although it has been 'glorified for hundreds of years', as 'the most relentless adversary of thought'[6] – the capital of philosophical authority held by the Kantian tradition. This masterly strategy enables the neo-Kantians to be attacked, but in the name of Kantianism, and thus combines the benefits of attacking orthodox Kantianism with those of claiming a Kantian authority: which is far from negligible in a field where all legitimacy emanates from Kant.

Cassirer, who was one of the prime targets, recognized what was happening; during the Davos debate, he allowed his academic 'distinction' to lapse and spoke the crudely reductive language of appropriation and monopoly:[7] 'Where Kantian philosophy is concerned, no one can claim with tranquil and dogmatic certainty to possess it already; everyone must take every opportunity to *reappropriate* it. In Heidegger's book, we are faced with an attempt at this kind of *reappropriation* of the fundamental position of Kant' (E. Cassirer, M. Heidegger, *Débat sur le kantisme et la philosophie, Davos, mars 1929*; my emphasis). The ambiguity of the word 'reappropriation' is significant in itself. It is explained later on: 'Here Heidegger is no longer speaking as a commentator, but as a pretender who takes up arms against Kant's system, so to speak, in order to overpower it and force it to serve his own problematics. Faced with this usurpation, we must demand restitution' (p. 74). It is still a metaphor, but one which will soon become more explicit: 'Heidegger has but one thought in his head, throughout his interpretation of Kant; there is no doubt about it, it is to liquidate that neo-Kantianism which would subordinate the whole of the Kantian system to the critique of knowledge, or even reduce it definitively to no more than a critique of knowledge. He sets against this the fundamentally metaphysical character of Kant's problematics' (p. 75). And further: 'Is Heidegger's hypothesis not after all an offensive strategy; do we not perhaps find ourselves no longer in the domain of an *analysis* of Kantian thought, but already caught up in the domain of a *polemic* against that thought?' (p. 78; my emphasis). Heidegger rejects Cassirer's tendentious analysis with a typically skilful negation: 'My intention was not to counter an "epistemological" interpretation with the novelty of one flattering the imagination' (p. 43).

Heidegger's reinterpretation of Kantianism is inseparable from his reinterpretation of phenomenology and his 'overcoming' of Husserl's thought: Kant (reinterpreted) is used to overcome Husserl, who, from another angle, enables him to overcome Kant. The purely phenomenological problem of the relation between pure experience, as an intuition of prepredicative objectivity, and judgement, as a formal intuition which founds the validity of the synthesis, finds in the theory of transcendental imagination the solution which Husserl was unable to provide because of his decision to limit himself to the quest for a transcendental logic (although it was his revelation that the act of knowledge cannot be divorced from temporality which led the way towards achieving that insight). The failure of Husserl's attempt to reconcile a Platonic conception of essences with a Kantian conception of transcendental subjectivity is overcome in Heidegger's ontology of temporality, that is, of transcendental finitude, which excludes the eternal from the horizon of human existence and which places at the source of judgement and the foundation of the theory of knowledge not an intellectual intuition but a finite, sensory intuition. The truth of phenomenology, which phenomenology is unaware of, and the truth of the *Critique of Pure Reason*, which the neo-Kantians have obscured, reside in the fact that 'to know, primitively, is to intuit'. Transcendental subjectivity, in as much as it transcends itself in order to create the possibility of the objectifying encounter, the opening up towards other entities, is nothing but time, whose source is in the imagination, and which thus constitutes the source of Being *qua* Being.

The reversal is radical: Husserl too related Being to time, truth to history, and, through the question of the origins of geometry, for example, he posed in relatively clear terms the problem of the history of the constitution of truth, but on 'terms' which were those of a defence of reason, and of philosophy as a rigorous science; Heidegger turns Being in time into the source of Being itself, and, steeping truth in history and its relativity, founds a (paradoxical) ontology of immanent historicity, a historicist ontology.[8] In Husserl's case, the task is to save reason at all costs; in Heidegger's case, reason is called radically into question, since historicity, a source of relativity and therefore of scepticism, is placed at the very origins of knowledge.

But things are never so simple, and the strategy of radical overcoming leads to fundamentally ambiguous (or, strictly speaking, *reversible*) positions, which will later facilitate non-contradictory reversals and meaningfully ambiguous dual-purpose tactics. By inscribing history within Being, by constituting authentic subjectivity as finitude assumed and thereby absolute, by installing at the heart of the constitutive 'Cogito' an ontological and constitutive (that is, deconstitutive) ontological time, Heidegger intends to overthrow Kant's overthrow of metaphysics, and he undertakes a metaphysical critique of all critiques of metaphysics; in short, he accomplishes the 'conservative revolution' (*die konservative Revolution*) in philosophy. And this he achieves through a strategy typical of the 'conservative revolutionaries' (and particularly

of Jünger): the strategy which consists in jumping into the fire
to avoid being burnt, to change everything without changing
anything, through one of those *heroic extremes* which, in the
drive to situate oneself always beyond the beyond, unite and
reconcile opposites *verbally*, in paradoxical, and magical,
propositions. Thus we find in Heidegger the statement that
metaphysics can only be a metaphysics of finitude, and that
only finitude leads to the unconditioned; or again, that existence is not temporal because it is historical, but is historical,
on the contrary, because it is temporal.[9]

Here one might well analyse the relation between Heidegger
and Hegel, as enunciated in *Identity and Difference* (tr. Joan
Stambaugh, New York, Harper & Row, 1960), where the confrontation takes the form of an annexation/distancing
through inversion of symbols: Being ceases to be an absolute
Concept, a complete conceptualization of all entities, and
becomes difference from any particular entities, becomes difference *qua* difference; the reconciliation of thought and
Being in the logos is realized, in Heidegger, in silence. It is the
task of making Being manifest, that is, of displaying the dialectic of the contradictions whereby the Void of pure Being
enables its transformation into a history of Becoming, which,
in the later Heidegger, becomes an effort to reveal as it were
the absence of Being and to display, in a sort of *negative
ontology* (in the sense in which we speak of a negative theology), the process of emanation of Being in the difference of
entities, an inversion of the *Selbstbewegung* of the Hegelian
Absolute which can only express itself in silence or in a poetic
evocation of the *Ens absconditum*.

The verbal somersault which allows escape from historicism
by asserting the essential historicity of the existing, and by
inscribing history and temporality within Being, that is, within
the ahistorical and the eternal, is the paradigm of all the
philosophical strategies of the conservative revolution in
philosophical matters. These strategies are always grounded in

a radical overcoming which allows everything to be preserved behind the appearance of everything changing, by joining opposites in a two-faced system of thought, which is therefore *impossible to circumvent*, since, like Janus, it is capable of facing challenges from all directions at once: the systematic extremism of essential thought enables it to overcome the most radical theses, whether these spring from the left or the right, by moving to a pivotal point where right becomes left, and vice versa.

Thus, to seek to use history, which is the source of relativism and nihilism, in order to overcome nihilism, is in fact to keep historicist ontology sheltered from history, by using the eternalization of temporality and of history in order to avoid the historicization of the eternal.[10] In giving an 'ontological basis' to temporal existence, Heidegger is *playing with fire*, by coming close to creating a historicist vision of the transcendental ego, which would give a real role to history by taking into account the process of the empirical constitution of the cognitive subject (as analysed by the positive social sciences)[11] and of the constitutive role of time and historical process in the genesis of 'essences' (those of geometry, for instance); but he also maintains a radical *difference* from any kind of anthropology 'which studies man as an object given in advance',[12] and even from the more 'critical' forms of philosophical anthropology (and especially those formulated by Cassirer or Scheler). Thus, in the very act of authorizing the reduction of truth to time, history, and the finite, and thereby depriving scientific truth of the eternity which it claims and which is granted by classical philosophy, this ontologization of history and time (like the ontologization of *Verstehen* which goes with it) snatches from history (and anthropological science) the right to claim eternal truth as ontological foundation of *Dasein* in temporalization and historicity, and claims for itself the status of *a priori* and eternal principle of all history (in the sense both of Heidegger's *Historie* and of his *Geschichte*). It founds the transhistorical truth of the philosophy which,

beyond all historical determination, enunciates the transhistorical truth of *Dasein* as historicity. But in establishing
historicity or understanding as the fundamental structure of
Dasein, through a founding tautology which leaves things
undisturbed – for we might well ask how the ontology of
understanding (*Verstehen*) makes understanding any easier to
understand – Heidegger may indeed give the impression that
he is formulating the question more fundamentally and radically, but in fact he suggests, without needing to express the
argument, that the positive sciences cannot have the last word
on the subject.

We can see a practical example of this philosophical 'line' in
the strategy which Heidegger deploys against Cassirer's *Philosophy of Symbolic Forms* during the Davos debate: having
declared at the outset that the genesis of neo-Kantianism is to
be explained by 'the embarrassment of philosophy when
forced to ask itself what, within the whole domain of knowledge, it may still claim as its own preserve' (*Débat sur le
kantisme*, (pp. 28–9), he shakes the foundations of the
epistemological ambition to found the social sciences,
although he approves in this ambition, of course, its respect of
the intellectual hierarchy: Cassirer's work, he says, 'takes to a
fundamentally superior level the problematic of positive
research in mythology' and offers a conception of myth
which, if it inspires empirical research, will provide a very
powerful *guiding* light able to illuminate and analyse new
facts, as it should also elaborate *in depth* the data already
acquired' (p. 94; my emphasis). Once he has uttered the profession of solidarity incumbent on representatives of a *dominant discipline* when they confront inferior disciplines,
Heidegger resorts to his favourite strategy, the *Wesentlichkeit*
move, with its insuperable overcoming of all overcoming, its
self-founding foundation of all foundation, its absolute prem-
iss to all premisses: 'is the previous determination of myth as
a constitutive function of consciousness sufficiently founded
itself? Where are the bases of such an obviously inevitable
foundation? Are these bases themselves sufficiently elabo-

rated?' And, after recalling the limits of the Kantian interpretation of the Copernican revolution, he continues: 'Is it
possible to purely and simply *"expand"* the critique of pure
reason into a critique of culture? Is it therefore so sure, or is
it not rather most contestable, that the foundations of the
Kantian transcendental interpretation of "culture" are explicitly clarified and founded?' (p. 95; my emphasis). This long,
meditative interrogation would merit quoting in its entirety:
the pure intention of overcoming through a 'founding
thought' becomes reinforced with the opposition, which
works as a *generative structure*, between the 'broad' (therefore
superficial and 'clear') and the 'profound', and is realized in a
half-incantatory, half-terroristic rhetoric of the *fundamental*
(its lexical proliferation including 'the profound', 'fundamental', 'foundation', 'founding', 'to found', 'to be
founded', 'profoundly', 'bases') and the *'prefatory'* ('is it
then so certain . . .', 'what should we think of the . . .',
'before we ask ourselves', 'it is only then that . . .', 'the
fundamental problem has not yet been broached'). This
foundation of the foundation, contrary to what we might
expect from this sceptical enquiry into the foundations of
Kantian subjectivity and its spiritualist vocabulary ('consciousness' , 'life', 'spirit', 'reason') should obviously not be
sought in the material conditions of existence of the producers
of the mythical discourse. 'Foundational' thought does not
want to acknowledge this 'vulgar', that is vulgarly 'empirical',
foundation.[13] 'Existential idealism' (as Gurvitch so rightly
calls it) only approaches existence in order to better distance
itself from the material conditions of existence: choosing, as
always, 'the inner way', *den Weg nach Innen*, as it was
described in the *völkisch* tradition, it seeks the foundation of
'mythical thought' in a 'preliminary elaboration of the ontological constitution of existence in general' (p. 97).

At the cost of a radical diminution of the significance of
what Kant called that 'arrogant word ontology', Heidegger
drew up the ontological structure of *Dasein* with existential
characteristics (also designated as 'fundamental existentials'

or 'fundamental modes of Being or Being-there'), described as the transcendental conditions (now to be called the ontological conditions) necessary for knowledge (as understanding, but also as language). Thus, through this ontologization of the transcendental, Heidegger achieves a first fusion of opposites, managing to render his position elusive, and unassimilable to either of the opposing positions. The confusion is increased by the fact that transcendental ontology defines Cognitive Being as a state of 'non-Being', or rather, as a temporalizing act or project, and thus the transcendental is completely ontologized by means of the ontologization of history, whereby Being is made identical with time. It is not difficult to see how Heidegger's famous reversal (*Kehre*), and his departure from the transcendental ontology and existential analytics of *Sein und Zeit*, were able to lead quite naturally, through the ontologization of history, to the negative ontology which, identifying Being with what Being is in so far as it presents itself to *Dasein*, refers to Being as a process of emergence (one cannot help thinking of Bergson's 'creative evolution' . . .) depending for its materialization on the thought which allows it to be, on *Gelassenheit* as submission to historicity.

Thus we find that there is no need even to establish a direct relation between Heidegger's 'reversal' and his semi-retirement after his period as Rector, to understand that the ultra-radicalism of this revolution in thought finds its apotheosis, once the moment of 'resolute commitment' has passed, in a sort of neo-Thomist wisdom, reminding everyone to 'recognize what is' and to 'live according to their condition': 'Shepherds live invisibly and outside the deserts of the desolated earth, which is only supposed to be of use for the guarantee of the dominance of man. . . . The unnoticeable law of the earth preserves the earth *in the sufficiency of* the emerging and perishing of all things *in the allotted sphere of the possible* which *everything follows*, and yet nothing knows. The birch tree never oversteps its possibility. The colony of bees dwells in its possibility. *It is first the will which arranges itself everywhere in technology* that devours the earth in the exhaustion and consumption and change of what is *artificial*'.[14]

That having been said, the academic and political reverberations of his pure thought were never entirely muted, whether in the philosophical field or beyond it. We only have to analyse Heidegger's philosophical positions, and those of the theorists he engaged in dialogue, in terms of the logic of the academic field or the political field, to perceive the specifically political implications of his most purely theoretical options. These secondary meanings have no need to be intended as such, since they are secreted automatically by the *metaphorical* correspondences, dual meanings, and hints which, because of the homology between the fields, arise from the application in the philosophical field of a much more generally valid 'line', that of the *habitus*, which orientates the ethical and political choices of 'empirical' and theoretical existence. Thus we immediately see that granting priority to philosophy over science and to intuition over judgement and concepts, which is one of the issues at stake in the confrontation between Heidegger and neo-Kantianism and in the struggle to push Kant either towards logic and reason, or on the contrary, towards Aesthetics and imagination, resounds in direct harmony with the displays of irrationalism which may be observed in the political field. By tending to subordinate reason to sensibility, to 'sensibilize reason' (like Schopenhauer, who rejected the Kantian distinction between intuition and concepts and found in intuition the source of all knowledge), the Heideggerian reading of the *Critique of Pure Reason* makes Kantianism look like a fundamental critique of the *Aufklärung* [Enlightenment].

We find the same effect when Heidegger applies to the religious, and more specifically the Lutheran, or para-religious tradition (like Kierkegaard's thought), the strategy of radical overcoming by means of 'essentialist' or 'foundational' thought which he had applied to the philosophy most dedicated to marking the break between religion and philosophy,

that of Kant. Heidegger introduces into philosophy a secularized form of the religious themes which the anti-theological
theology of Kierkegaard had already translated into metaphysical theses: these are, for instance, the notion of *Schuld*
(guilt), constituted as the mode of being of *Dasein*, or so many
other concepts of the same origins or colouring, *Angst*
(anxiety), *Absturz* (fall), *Verderbnis* (corruption), *verfallen*
(to deteriorate), *Versuchung* (temptation), *Geworfenheit*
(dereliction), *Innerweltlichkeit* (within-the-world-liness), etc.
    We might follow Heidegger's tendency to play on words
and say that essentialist thought (*das wesentliche Denken*)
concentrates on essentials. By constituting as 'modes of being
of *Dasein*' barely euphemized substitutes for theological
notions, it inscribes within Being all the features of the 'ordinary' condition of 'ordinary' man: being abandoned in the
'world', experiencing 'loss of self' in the 'worldliness' of
'gossip', 'curiosity' and 'ambiguity'. The truth of this metaphysics of the 'fall', which makes 'errance', as a kind of
original sin, the source of all particular errors, from forgetfulness of Being to worship of banality, is resumed and exposed
in the strategy of annexation – very like that which Heidegger
directed against the neo-Kantians – through which alienation
(*Entfremdung*), reduced to the *völkisch* sense of 'uprooting',
finds itself constituted as the 'ontologico-existential structure'
of *Dasein*, that is as ontological deficiency. But, apart from its
political function as a *sociodicy* towards the ontologization of
history, this strategic borrowing reveals the truth of that other
typically Heideggerian effect, the (artificial) radical overcoming of all possible radicalism, which provides conformism
with its most water-tight justification. To identify ontological
alienation as the foundation of all alienation, is, in a manner
of speaking, to banalize and yet simultaneously dematerialize
both economic alienation and any discussion of this alienation, by a radical but imaginary overcoming of any revolutionary overcoming.
    Heidegger reintroduces into the domain of academically

acceptable philosophical thought (and his debate with the neo-Kantians is a considerable help in ensuring him this respectability) topics and modes of expression – and in particular an incantatory and prophetic style – which were previously confined to those sects, encamped on the margins of the field of academic philosophy, where Nietzsche and Kierkegaard, George and Dostoevsky, political mysticism and religious fervour, met and mingled. In so doing, he produces a previously impossible philosophical position, which is situated in relation to marxism and neo-Kantianism in the way that the 'conservative revolutionaries' are situated in the ideologico-political field in relation to the socialists and the liberals.[15] And nothing provides better evidence of this homology – apart from direct borrowings on the most overtly political questions, like that of technology – than the privileged place allotted to *resoluteness* (*Entschlossenheit*), that free and almost desperate confrontation of existential limits, which is equally opposed to rational mediation and dialectical transcendence.

4

Censorship and the imposition of form

Heidegger's writing is an exemplary manifestation of the amount of work which has to be accomplished by the unconscious as well as the conscious mind, if the expressive drive is to be contained within the limits imposed by the censorship which any cultural field exerts through its very structure. The philosophical problematic as a space of objectively realized possibilities functions as a *possible market*, exercising effects of repression, or licensing and encouragement, on the expressive drive. Each producer must come to terms with this problematic, and it is only within the limits of the constraints which it imposes that his social phantasms are able to find expression. Consequently, learned discourse may be considered as a 'compromise formation' in the Freudian sense, that is as the product of a transaction between, on the one hand, the expressive drives, themselves determined by the positions in the field which their speakers hold, and, on the other hand, the structural constraints of the field where the discourse is produced and exchanged, and which functions as censorship.[1] The work of *euphemization* and sublimation, which is both conscious and unconscious, and which is necessary in order to *render speakable* the most inadmissible expressive drives in a given state of censorship in the field, implies *imposing form* [*mettre en forme*] as well as *observing formalities* [*mettre des formes*]; the success of this work and the profit which it can provide in any given state of the structures of opportunity for material or symbolic profit that are the medium of censorship, depend on the specific capital of the producer, that is on his specific authority and competence.

The transactions and compromises which constitute the work of imposing form can never be entirely imputed to the conscious aims of a rational calculation of the material or symbolic costs and profits. And the most powerful *rhetorical effects* are the product of the intersection, which is never entirely controlled by the conscious mind, of two immanent necessities: the necessity of a *habitus*, more or less completely geared towards maintaining the position held in the field, and the necessity immanent within a particular state of the field. This latter necessity influences practices by means of objective mechanisms, such as those which work to restore equilibrium between the position and the dispositions of its holder, or those engendered almost automatically through homologies between different fields, by the effects of overdetermination and euphemization able to endow discourse with an opacity and a polyphonic complexity inaccessible to even the most expert rhetorical strategists.

Cultural products owe their most specific properties to the social conditions of their production and more precisely to the position of the producer in the field of production, which dictates, albeit through divergent mediatory processes, not only the expressive drive, and the form and force of the censorship which affects it, but also the competence which enables this drive to be satisfied within the framework of these constraints. The dialectical relation which is established between the expressive drive and the structural censorship of the field prevents us from distinguishing in the *opus operatum* the form from the content, what is being said from the manner of saying it or even the manner of hearing it. By imposing form, the censorship exercised by the structure of the field determines its discursive form – although formalist analysts always attempt to divorce this from social determinisms – and, inextricably, its content which is indissociable from its appropriate expression, and therefore literally unthinkable outside the acknowledged norms and accredited forms. Censorship also determines the forms of reception: to produce a philosophical discourse of a duly formal nature, that is, cloaked in the apparatus of signs, syntax, lexicon, references, etc., in which we recognize the philosophical nature of a discourse, and which a discourse exploits in order to declare its philosophical nature,[2] is to produce a product which requires to be received with due formality, that is with due respect for the forms it has adopted, or, as we see in literature, *in terms of pure form*. Legitimate works are thus able to exercise a violence which shelters them from the violence which would be needed if we were to perceive the expressive drive that they express only in forms which deny it: the histories of art, literature, and philosophy bear witness to the efficiency of the strategies of imposition of form through which consecrated works dictate the terms of their own perception.

A work is attached to a specific field as much by its form as its content: if we try to imagine what Heidegger would have said in another form, that of philosophical discourse as it was practised in Germany in 1890, or that of the social science paper as published nowadays at Yale or Harvard, we are bound to imagine an *impossible* Heidegger (for example, a philosophical 'vagrant', or an oppositional emigrant, in 1933) or a field of production just as impossible in the Germany of the time when Heidegger was active. The form through which symbolic productions participate most directly in the social conditions of their production is also the one through which they exercise their most specific social effect: symbolic violence properly speaking can only be exercised by the person who exercises it – and suffered by the person who suffers it – in a form which makes it misrecognizable as such, that is makes it recognizable as legitimate.

Scholarly discourse, the special languages which bodies of specialists (philosophers, jurists, etc.) produce and reproduce through systematic distortions of the common language, are distinguished from scientific language in that they conceal heteronomy behind the appearance of autonomy: since they are unable to function without the assistance of ordinary language, they must produce the illusion of independence by *staging an artificial break*, using different procedures according to the fields, or, within the same field, according to different positions and moments. They can for instance mimic the fundamental property of all scientific language, the determination of an element through its belonging to a system.[3] Thus the properly Heideggerian concepts which are borrowings from ordinary language are transfigured by the process of imposing form which severs them from their common usage by inserting them, through the systematic accentuation of morphological relations, into a network of relations displayed in the concrete form of the language, and by thus suggesting that each element of the discourse depends on the others *simultaneously* as signifier and signified. In this way a word as ordinary as *Fürsorge*, solicitude, becomes *palpably* attached by its very form to a whole set of words of the same family, *Sorge*, care, *Sorgfalt*, carefulness, solicitude, *Sorglosigkeit*, carelessness, negligence, *sorgenvoll*, concerned, *besorgt*, preoccupied, *Lebenssorge*, concern for life, *Selbstsorge*, self-interest.

When Gadamer, in the review already mentioned, attributes to me the idea that there exists a 'true sense' of words and that in the case of the word *Fürsorge*, the sense of social welfare is the 'only legitimate one' according to me, he misses what is the very core of my analysis: firstly, the fact that words and discourse in general only receive their complete determination, including their sense and value, in their pragmatic relations with a field which functions as a market. Secondly, he overlooks the polysemic or rather the *polyphonic* character which

Heidegger's discourse owes to its author's peculiar ability to speak for several fields and several markets at once. The error consists in attributing to me the philosophy of language and of the typically philologistic interpretation which is expressed literally by his teacher, Heidegger: 'The real signification of "discourse", which is obvious enough, gets constantly covered up by the later history of the word *logos*, and especially by the numerous and arbitrary Interpretations which subsequent philosophy has provided' (*Being and Time* (Oxford, Blackwell, 1962), p. 55). In fact, it is as naïve to wonder what the true sense of words is, as it is to wonder, in Austin's terms, what the 'real colour of the chameleon is' (J. L. Austin, *Sense and Sensibilia* (Oxford, Oxford University Press, 1962), p. 66): there are as many meanings as there are different usages and markets. Another error of reading, which also has its source in the fact of projecting one's own philosophy into the work analysed, makes Gadamer say that the rhetorical intention is exclusive of the intention of truth – and in this case, one might also note that it involves a simplistic definition of rhetoric, albeit one deriving from Plato and Aristotle. In fact, we are again faced with the problem of the colour of the chameleon. Gadamer, following orthodox scientific opinion, tacitly accepts the idea that rhetoric is opposed as something calculated, artificial, and self-conscious to some natural, spontaneous, primary, primitive mode of expression. This is to forget that an expressive drive can only be fulfilled through a relation with a market and that there are thus as many *rhetorics* as there are markets; that the ordinary uses of language (whose diversity one negates by speaking of 'ordinary language', as philosophers of language do) deploy kinds of rhetoric which may be highly refined without being conscious and calculated; and also that the most refined versions of learned rhetoric, those used by Heidegger for instance, do not necessarily suppose calculation of, or complete control over, the effects deployed.

Because of its frequency in sayings and proverbs enshrining popular wisdom, the play on words which show a 'family resemblance' through their etymological or morphological relation is only one of the means, if doubtless the most reliable, of giving the impression that there is a necessary relation between two signifieds. The association through alliteration or assonance which establishes quasi-material relations of resemblance of form and sound can bring to light hidden relations between signifieds, or even make them exist through the sheer play of forms: this is the case, for instance, with the philosophical word games of the later Heidegger, *Denken* = *Danken* (thinking = thanking), although its magic is somewhat diluted, to the chagrin of his Gallic disciples, if translated into French (*penser* = *remercier*); or the snowballing puns on *Sorge als besorgende Fürsorge*, 'caring as careful procuration', which might be labelled verbal flannel if the network of morphological allusions and etymological references did not produce the illusion of a global coherence of form, and therefore of sense, and, thus, of the appearance of an apparently self-evident discourse: '*Die Entschlossenheit aber ist nur in der Sorge gesorgte und als Sorge mögliche Eigentlichkeit dieser selbst*' (Resoluteness, however, is only that authenticity which, in care, is the object of care, and which is possible as care – the authenticity of care itself).[4]

All the potential resources of language are deployed to give the impression that there exists a necessary link between all the signifiers, and that the relation between the signifiers and the signifieds is only established through the mediation of the system of philosophical concepts, 'technical' words which are ennobled forms of ordinary words (*Entdeckung*, discovery/ uncovering, and *Entdecktheit*, discovered-ness/uncovered-ness), traditional notions (like *Dasein*) but used slightly out of focus in order to signal their *distance*, neologisms made to measure so as to constitute distinctions allegedly unthought, or at least to produce an impression of radical overcoming (existentiel and existential; *zeitlich*, timely, and *temporal*, temporal, an opposition which moreover has no significant impact in *Sein und Zeit*).

Imposing form produces the illusion of systematic order,

and, through the break with ordinary language thus effected, the illusion of an autonomous system. By inserting the word *Fürsorge* into a network of words both morphologically similar and etymologically related, and so weaving it into the tissue of his lexical fabric, Heidegger tears the word away from its ordinary sense, the one which is unambiguously given in the expression *Sozialfürsorge*, social welfare: once transformed and transfigured, it loses its common identity, and cloaks itself in a distorted sense (which might be rendered more or less by the word 'procuration', taken in its etymological sense). At the end of this process of distortion, worthy of the conjuror who draws attention to something unimportant in order to distract our attention from what he has to hide, the social phantasm of (social) assistance, symbol of the 'Welfare State' or the 'Insurance State', which Carl Schmitt or Ernst Jünger denounce in a less euphemistic language, can inhabit or haunt legitimate discourse (*Sorge* and *Fürsorge* are at the heart of the theory of temporality), but in such a form that they do not seem to do so, that they do not in fact do so.

Where the ordinary process of euphemization substitutes one word (often of contradictory meaning) for another, or visibly neutralizes the ordinary meaning either by an explicit caution (inverted commas, for instance) or by a distinctive definition, Heidegger proceeds by establishing a network of morphologically interconnected words, within which the ordinary word, at once identical and transfigured, receives a new identity: thus he invites a philological and polyphonic reading, able to evoke and revoke the ordinary meaning simultaneously, able to suggest it while ostensibly repressing it, along with its pejorative connotations, into the order of vulgar and vulgarly 'anthropological' comprehension.[5]

The philosophical imagination, like mythical or poetic thought, takes delight in superimposing the phenomenal relation of sound on an essential relation of sense, and in playing with linguistic forms which are also classificatory forms: thus, in *Vom Wesen der Wahrheit*, the opposition between the 'essence' (*Wesen*) and 'non-essence' or 'in-essence' (*Unwesen*) is underpinned with the surreptitious opposition, simultaneously evoked and revoked, between order – a sort of phantom term, which is absent, yet present *in effigy* – and *disorder*, one of the possible meanings of *Un-wesen*. The series of parallel oppositions, which are unevenly euphemized variants of the limited number of 'primordial' oppositions, themselves roughly reducible to each other, numerous examples of which may be found throughout Heidegger's work subsequent to his 'reversal', restate the founding opposition, which is itself subject to taboo, but they do so in sublimated form – a form all the more universal in its applications for being more difficult to recognize (like the opposition between the ontic and the ontological). In so doing, they constitute that opposition as an absolute, by inscribing it within Being at the same time as denying it symbolically.

It is its incorporation into the system of philosophical language that facilitates the *negation* [or *Verneinung*, in Freudian terms] of the primary sense, the sense which the taboo word takes from its reference to the system of ordinary language and which, although officially banished from the overt system, continues to lead a subterranean existence. This negation is the source of the double standards authorized by the dual message registered in each discursive element always informed simultaneously by two systems, the overt system of the philosophical idiolect and the latent system of ordinary language, or belonging, in other words, to two mental spaces which are indissociable from two social spaces. Submitting the expressive drive to the transformation necessary for it to accede to the order of what is sayable in a given field, prising it away from the unsayable and the unnamable, implies more than just substituting one, acceptable word for another, censored one. For this elementary form of euphemization hides another, which consists in using the essential property of language, according to Saussure's conflictive model of the primacy of relations over elements and form over substance, in order to disguise the repressed elements by inserting them into a network of relations which modify their *value* without modifying their 'substance'. It is only with specialized languages, produced by specialists with the explicit intention of creating a system, that the effect of disguise through the imposition of form is fully operational: in this case, as in all cases of camouflage through form, the meanings marked as taboo, although theoretically recognizable, remain misrecognized in practice; although they are present as substance, they are, like a face hidden in a join-the-dots puzzle, absent as form. The role of this kind of expression is to mask the *primitive experiences of the social world* and the *social phantasms* which are its source, as much as to disclose them; to allow them to speak, while using a mode of expression which suggests that they are not being said. These specialized languages can enunciate such experience only in forms of expression which render them unrecognizable, because the specialist is unable to acknowledge that he is enunciating them. As it is submitted to the tacit or explicit norms of a particular field, the primitive substance dissolves, so to speak, in the form. This imposition of form is at once transformation and transubstantiation: the substance signified *is* the significant form in which it is realized.

Through the imposition of form it becomes both just and unjustified to reduce the negation to what it negates, to the social phantasm which is its source. Because of the fact that this *Verneinung* (which Freud, using a Hegelian term, calls a 'lifting [*Aufhebung*] of repression') simultaneously maintains and denies both the repression and what is repressed, it doubles the benefit, adding to the advantage of speaking the profit of denying what is said, through the manner of saying it. Thus for example, the opposition between *Eigentlichkeit*, 'authenticity', and *Uneigentlichkeit*, 'inauthenticity', those 'primordial modes of Being-there', as Heidegger says, around

which the whole work is organized (even from the viewpoint of
the most strictly internal readings), is a particular and particularly subtle retranslation of the common opposition between
the 'elite' and the 'masses'. 'They', (*Das Man*, literally
'one') are tyrannical ('the real dictatorship of the "they"'),
inquisitorial ('they keep watch over everything'), and reduce
everything to the lowest level, the universal 'they' evade their
responsibilities, opt out of their liberty: they live on 'pro-
cured' assistance, fecklessly depending on society or the 'Welfare State' which, especially through 'social assistance'
(*Sozialfürsorge*), looks after them and cares for their future on
their behalf. One could list the commonplaces of academic
aristocratism which recur throughout this oft-commented
passage,[6] replete with topoi on the agora as an antithesis of the
scholè, leisure versus school. There is a hatred of statistics
(harping on the theme of the 'average') seen as a symbol of all
the operations of 'levelling down' which threaten the 'person'
(here called *Dasein*) and its most precious attributes, its 'originality' and its 'privacy'. There is a contempt for all forces
which 'level down', doubtless with a particular disgust for
egalitarian ideologies which endanger 'everything gained by a
struggle', meaning culture (the specific capital of the mandarin, who is the son of his works), ideologies which encourage
the masses to 'take things easily and make them easy'. There
is also a revolt against social mechanisms such as those of
opinion, the hereditary enemy of the philosopher, which
recurs here through the play on *Öffentlichkeit* and *Öffentlich*,
'public opinion' and 'public', and against anything symbol-
izing 'social assistance', that is democracy, political parties,
paid holidays (as a breach in the monopoly of the *scholè* and
meditation in the forest), 'culture for the masses', television,
and Plato in paperback.[7] Heidegger was to say this so much
better, in his inimitable *pastoral* style, when, in his *Introduction to Metaphysics*, written in 1935, he set out to show
how the triumph of the scientifico-technological spirit in
Western civilization is accomplished and perfected in the

'flight of the gods, the destruction of the earth, the transformation of men into a mass, the hatred and suspicion of
everything free and creative' (*die Flucht der Götter, die
Zerstörung der Erde, die Vermassung des Menschen, der
Vorrang des Mittelmässigen*).[8]

This play with the tangible forms of language attains its
most accomplished form when it is brought to bear not on
isolated words but on pairs of terms, that is on relations
between contradictory terms. As opposed to simple philosophical puns based on assonance or alliteration, the 'primordial' puns, those which orientate and organize his thought
in depth, play on verbal form to exploit both its sensory
patterning and its classificatory structures. These total forms,
which reconcile the independent necessities of sound and sense
in the miracle of a twice necessary expression, are the transformed form of a linguistic fabric which is already politically
infiltrated, in that it is interwoven with structured alternatives, recorded and preserved in ordinary language, which are
already objectively political. The predilection of all learned
languages for *binary thinking* is not to be otherwise explained:
what is censored and repressed, in this case, is not a taboo term
taken in an isolated state, but an oppositional relation between
words, which always refers back to an oppositional relation
between social positions or social groups.

Ordinary language is not only an infinite reserve of tangible
forms available for poetical or philosophical games or, as in
the later Heidegger and his successors, for free associations
around what Nietzsche called a *Begriffsdichtung*; it is also
a reservoir of forms of apperception of the social world,
of commonplaces which enshrine the principles of vision of
the social world common to a whole group (Germanic versus
Celtic or Latin, ordinary versus distinguished, etc.). The structure of the social world is only ever named and apprehended
through forms of classification which, even when they are
those mobilized by ordinary language, are never independent
of that structure (which is always forgotten in *formalist*

analyses of these forms): indeed, although the most socially 'marked' oppositions (vulgar/distinguished) may receive very different meanings according to usage and users, ordinary language, produced by the accumulated process of a thought dominated by the power relations between classes, and *a fortiori* scholarly language, which is produced in fields wracked by the interests and values of the dominant classes, are in a way primary ideologies, which lend themselves 'quite naturally' to uses conforming to the values and interests of the dominant classes.[9] By converting the dichotomies and schemata of ordinary thinking into metaphorical terms, politics may be converted into ontology. But the metaphorical process whereby this metaphysics is engendered leads not from things visible to things invisible, but from the latent and possibly unconscious content to the declared content of discourse. As transfers from one space to another, the function of these metaphors is to link the two spaces which the artificial break introduced by the thesis of ontological difference officially declared to be separate, and they also arrange for the founding oppositions to be *preserved* and surreptitiously continue to underpin discourse.

Among philosophically distinguished spirits the opposition between the distinguished and the vulgar cannot be enunciated in vulgar terms: Heidegger has too refined a sense of philosophical distinction for even his political writings to yield 'naïvely' political theses; and there is abundant evidence of his intention to distinguish himself from the most obvious forms of Nazi ideology.[10] The opposition which we might call 'primary' – in both senses – is to be found in his work only in the highly censored form of philosophemes functioning as euphemisms, which will be constantly transfigured, as his otherwise static system progresses, in a series of different, but equally sublimated, guises.

The imposition of form serves in itself as a warning: it camps on the heights in order to express its sovereign distance from all determinations, even from those 'isms' which reduce the irreducible unity of a thought system to the uniformity of a logical class; and also its distance from all determinisms, especially social ones, which reduce the priceless individuality of a thinker to the banality of a class. It is this distance, this *difference*, which becomes explicitly established at the heart of a philosophical discourse, cutting across the opposition between the ontological and the ontic (or the anthropological) and which provides the previously euphemized discourse with a second, and this time impregnable, defensive barrier: each word henceforth bears the indelible trace of the *break* which separates the authentically ontological sense from the ordinary and vulgar sense, and which is sometimes inscribed within the very signifying substance, through one of those phonological games so often imitated since (*existentiell/existential*).

This two-faced play on double-edged words finds its natural echo in the warnings against 'vulgar' and 'vulgarly anthropological' readings attempting to expose to broad daylight the meanings which are negated but not refuted, and which are translated by philosophical sublimation into the empty presence of a ghostly existence: 'The term "concern" has, in the first instance, its *colloquial signification* [vorwissenschaftliche = "prescientific"], and can mean to carry out something, to get it done [erledigen], to "straighten it out". It can also mean to provide oneself with something. We use the expression with still another characteristic turn of phrase when we say "I am concerned for the success of the undertaking". Here "concern" means something like apprehensiveness. *In contrast to these colloquial ontical significations, the expression "concern" will be used* in the present investigation *as an ontological term for an existentiale*, and will designate the Being of a possible way of Being-in-the-world. This term has been chosen not because Dasein happens to be proximally and to a large extent "practical" and economic, but because the Being of Dasein itself is to be made visible as care (*Sorge*). This expression too is to be taken as an *ontological structural* concept. It *has nothing to do* with "tribulation", "melancholy", or the "cares of life", though *ontically* one can come across these in every Dasein'.[11]

These cautionary strategies might have awakened the suspicions of non-German readers, if the latter had not been subject to conditions of reception which made it very unlikely that they would detect the hidden connotations, which are disowned in advance by Heidegger (all the more so since the translations 'suppress' them systematically in the name of the break between the ontical and the ontological). Indeed, in addition to the resistance to analysis offered by a work which is the product of such systematic strategies of euphemization there is also in this case one of the most pernicious effects of the exportation of cultural products, the disappearance of all the subtle signs of social or political origins, of all the often very discreet marks of the social importance of a discourse and the intellectual position of its author, in short, of all the infinitesimal features to which the native reader is obviously most vulnerable, but which he can apprehend better than others once he is equipped with techniques of objectification. We think for instance of all the 'administrative' connotations discovered by Adorno behind 'existential' terms like *Begegnung* (encounter), or words like *Anliegen* (concern) and *Auftrag* (commission), a pre-eminently ambiguous term, both 'the object of an administrative command' and a 'heartfelt wish', which was already the object of a deviant usage in Rilke's poetry (T. Adorno, *The Jargon of Authenticity*, trans. K. Tarnowski and F. Will (London: Routledge & Kegan Paul, 1986), pp. 77–88).

The imposition of a sharp divide between the sacred and the profane, which underpins the claims of any body of specialists, in ensuring a monopoly over a body of knowledge or a sacred practice by designating others as profane, thus takes on an original form: it is omnipresent, dividing each word against itself, as it were, by making it signify that it does not signify what it seems to signify – by placing it between inverted commas, or significantly distorting its substantive meaning, or sometimes just setting it etymologically or phonologically within a tendentious lexical cluster – and thus inscribing within it the distance which separates the 'authentic' sense from the 'vulgar' or 'naïve' sense.[12] By discrediting the primary significations which continue to function as a hidden support of a number of relations constitutive of the overt system, the initiates provide themselves with the means to double-cross any double-guessers of their double-dealing. Indeed, despite the anathema they attract, these negated meanings still fulfil a philosophical function, since they function at the very least as a negative referent against which we measure the philosophical and social distance separating the 'ontological' from the 'ontical', that is the initiated from the profane – whose ignorance or perversity is entirely responsible for any guilty evocation of vulgar meanings. In giving alternative significance to the words of Everyman, in reactivating the subtle truth, or *etumon*, which routine usage fails to grasp, one makes the success or failure of philologico-philosophical alchemy depend on the true relations between words: 'If an alchemist who is not an initiate in heart and soul fails in his experiments, it is not only because he is using impure elements, but above all because he uses the common *properties* of these impure elements in his thinking, instead of the *virtues* of the ideal elements. Thus, once we have achieved the complete and absolute duplication, we find ourselves plunged in the experience of *ideality*'.[13] Language, too, has its subtle elements, liberated by philologico-philosophical subtlety, such as the duplicity of the Greek word *on* [being], at once a noun and a verbal form, which leads Heidegger to say: 'What is here set forth, which at first may be taken for grammatical hair-splitting, is in truth the riddle of Being'.[14]

In this way, once we have faith in the effectiveness of philosophical negation, we can even exhume the censored meanings, and find a supplementary effect in the complete reversal of the relation between overt system and hidden system which is provoked by the *return of the repressed*: how could we possibly avoid noticing that the best evidence of the power of 'essential thought' is its talent for grounding in Being such realities as the derisively contingent 'social security', – objects so unworthy of thought that they are mentioned only between inverted commas?[15] Thus it comes to pass, in this 'upside-down world' where the event is never more than an illustration of the 'essence', that the foundation gets to be founded by what it founds.[16] 'For example, "*welfare work*" (Fürsorge), as an empirical *social arrangement*, is grounded in Dasein's state of Being as Being-with. Its empirical urgency gets its motivation in that Dasein maintains itself principally and most usually in the deficient modes of solicitude'.[17] The blatant but invisible reference, invisible because of its blatant-ness, helps to disguise the fact that *he has constantly been discussing social welfare* in an entire work *ostensibly* devoted to an ontological quality of Being-there whose 'empirical' (that is ordinary, vulgar, banal) 'need' for assistance is only a con-tingent event. The paradigm of the purloined letter, which Lacan illustrates with one of Freud's jokes: "If you say you're going to Cracow, you want me to believe you're going to Lemberg. But I know that in fact you're going to Cracow. So why are you lying to me?"[18] is perfectly exemplified in euphe-mized discourse, which tends to suggest, by emphasizing what it is really supposed to be stating, that it is not really saying what it has constantly been saying. In fact there is no doubt: social welfare, *Sozialfürsorge*, is precisely what 'cares for' those on welfare and 'on their behalf', what relieves them of caring for themselves, authorizing them to be careless, 'facile', and 'frivolous', just as the philosophical *Fürsorge*, the sublime version of the above, relieves *Dasein* of care or, to paraphrase Sartre's *Being and Nothingness* (1943), frees the 'pour-soi' [self-conscious being] from its freedom, plunging it into the 'bad faith' and 'serious-mindedness' of 'inauthentic' existence. 'Thus the particular Dasein in its everydayness is *disburdened* by the "they". Not only that; by thus disburdening it of its

Being, the "they" accommodates Dasein if Dasein has any tendency to *take things easily* and *make them easy*. And because the "they" constantly accommodates the particular Dasein by disburdening it of its Being, the "they" retains and enhances its stubborn dominion'.[19]

Everything is arranged so as to prohibit as indecent or ignorant any attempt to apply to the text the *violence* which is recognized by Heidegger himself as legitimate when he applies it to Kant, and which alone enables one to 'grasp the meaning beyond the obstinate silence of the language'. Any exposition of the originative thought which repudiates the inspired paraphrase of the untranslatable idiolect is condemned without trial by the guardians of the sanctuary.[20] The only way of saying what words *mean to say*, when they refuse to say innocently what they mean, or, alternatively, when they keep saying it but only indirectly, is to reduce the irreducible, to translate the untranslatable, to say what they mean in the naïve terms which their primary function is precisely to deny. 'Authenticity' is not a naïve designation of the exclusive quality of a social 'elite', it indicates a universal potential – as does 'inauthenticity' – yet this potential is only really accessible to those who manage to appropriate it by apprehending it for what it is, and by managing to 'tear themselves' away from 'inauthenticity', a sort of original sin, thus stigmatized as a fault guilty of its own failing, since the chosen few *are* capable of being converted. Which is clearly stated by Jünger: 'Whether to assume one's own destiny, or to be treated like an object: that is the dilemma which everyone, nowadays, is certain to have to resolve, but to have to decide alone. . . . Consider man in his pristine state of freedom, as created by God. He is not the exception, nor is he one of an elite. Far from it: for the free man is hidden within every man, and differences exist only in so far as each individual is able to develop that freedom which was his birthright'.[21] Although they are equal in their potential freedom, men are unequal in their ability to make authentic use of their freedom, and only an 'elite' can seize the opportunity offered by this universal potential and accede to the freedom of the 'elite'. This ethical voluntarism – which will be pushed to its limit by Sartre – converts the objective dualism of social destiny into a dualism of relations to existence, deriving authentic existence from 'an existential modification' of the ordinary way of apprehending everyday existence, that is, in plain speaking, a mental revolution.[22] Heidegger makes authenticity begin with the apprehension of inauthenticity, in the moment of truth where *Dasein* is revealed through anxiety as projecting order into the world through its decision (which is a sort of Kierkegaardian 'leap' into the unknown).[23] Contrariwise, he describes man's reduction to the state of an instrument as another 'way of apprehending everyday existence', the way which 'they' adopt when 'they' treat themselves as tools and 'care about' tools for their instrumental utility, and thus become instruments themselves, adapting themselves to others as an instrument adapts to other instruments, fulfilling a function which others could fulfil just as well and, once reduced in this way to the state of an interchangeable element in a set, forget themselves in the fulfilment of their function. When Heidegger discusses existence in terms of these alternatives, he reduces the objective dualism of social conditions to the dualism of the modes of existence which they obviously encourage very unequally; and he thereby considers both those who gain access to 'authentic' existence and those who 'abandon themselves' to 'inauthentic' existence to be responsible for what they are, either for their 'resoluteness'[24] in tearing themselves away from everyday existence in order to exploit their potential, or for their 'resignation', which dooms them to 'degradation' and 'social welfare'.

5

Internal readings and the respect of form

The 'elevated' style is not merely a contingent property of philosophical discourse. It is the means whereby a discourse signals itself as an authorized discourse which, by virtue of its very conformity, becomes invested with the authority of a body of people especially mandated to exercise a sort of conceptual magistrature (with its emphasis on logic or on ethics depending on the authors and the eras). In learned discourse as in ordinary speech, styles are ordered in hierarchies, but they also create hierarchies. For a thinker of high status an elevated language is appropriate: which is what made the 'unstylized pathos' of Heidegger's 1933 address seem sc inappropriate in the eyes of anyone who had a sense of philosophical dignity, that is of their dignity as philosophers; these were the same people who acclaimed as a philosophical event the philosophically stylized pathos of *Sein und Zeit*.[1]

It is through the 'elevated' style that the status of a discourse is invoked, as is the respect due to that status. One does not react to a sentence such as this: 'the real dwelling plight lies in this that mortals ever search anew for the nature of dwelling, that they must ever learn to dwell',[2] in the same way that one would react to a statement in ordinary language, such as this: 'the housing shortage is getting worse', or even a statement in technical language, such as 'On the Hausvogteiplatz, in one of the financial centres of Berlin, the price of building land per square metre rose from 115 Marks in 1865 to 344 Marks in 1880 and 990 Marks in 1895'.[3] As a formally constructed discourse, philosophical discourse dictates the conditions of its own perception. The imposition of form, which keeps the layman at a respectable distance, protects the text from 'trivialization' – as Heidegger calls it – by reserving it for an *internal reading*, in both senses, that of a reading confined within the bounds of the text itself, and, concomitantly, that of a reading reserved for the closed group of professional readers who accept as self-evident an 'internalist' definition of reading: we have only to observe social custom to see that the philosophical text is defined as one which can only (in fact) be read by 'philosophers', that is, by readers who are convinced in advance, and are ready to recognize and grant recognition to a philosophical discourse, and to read it as it requires to be read, that is 'philosophically', according to the pure and purely philosophical intentions of the philosopher, excluding all reference to anything other than the discourse itself, which, being its own foundation, admits of no outer dimensions.

The institutionalized circle of collective misreading which creates belief in the value of a discourse is only established when the structure of the field of production and circulation of this discourse is such that the *negation* which it operates (by saying what it has to say only in a form which tends to show that it is not saying it), encounters commentators able to *re-misread* the negated message; whereby what the form denies is re-misread – in other words, acknowledged and recognized in the form, and only in the form, which this self-denial creates. In short, a formally constructed discourse solicits a formal, or formalist, reading which recognizes and reproduces the initial negation, instead of denying it in order to dis-cover what it has been denying. The symbolic violence that any ideological discourse implies in its misreading, which demands re-misreading, is only operative in so far as it obtains the assent of its addressees to treat it as it wishes to be treated, that is with all the respect that it deserves, observing the proper formalities required by its formal properties. An ideological production is all the more successful as it is able to *put in the wrong* anyone who attempts to *reduce* it to its objective truth: enunciating the hidden truth of a discourse causes a scandal because it says something which was 'the last thing you should have said'.

It is remarkable, knowing how tenaciously he rejected and refuted any external or reductive readings of his work (letters to Jean Wahl, Jean Beaufret, to a student, to Richardson, discussion with a Japanese philosopher, etc.), that Heidegger had no hesitation in using the arguments of a 'clumsy socio-logism' against his rivals (as when criticizing Sartre's *Existentialism and Humanism* (1946)): thus, if necessary, he was prepared to reinvest the topic of the 'dictatorship of the public realm' with the strictly *social* (if not sociological) sense which it undoubtedly had in *Sein und Zeit*, and what is more, to do so in a passage where he is attempting precisely to establish that the 'existential analysis' of the 'they' 'in no way means to furnish an *incidental* contribution to sociology' (*Letter on Humanism* (1947), in *Basic Writings*, ed. D. F. Krell (London, Routledge & Kegan Paul, 1978), p. 197). This recycling of Heidegger I by Heidegger II bears witness to the fact (under-lined by the emphasis on 'incidental' in the sentence quoted) that Heidegger II has in no way repudiated Heidegger I.

The most refined symbolic strategies can never completely dictate the conditions of their own success and they would be bound to fail if they were unable to count on the active conniv-ance of a whole body of defenders of the faith who orchestrate and amplify the primary attack on reductive readings.[4] Thus it is that *The Letter on Humanism*, the most striking and the most often quoted of all the interventions aimed at strate-gically manipulating the relation between overt and latent systems, and thereby manipulating the public image of the work, had functioned like a sort of pastoral letter, an ever-flowing spring of commentaries enabling the lesser clergy of Being to reproduce on their own behalf the precautions inscribed within each of the master's warnings and thus to place themselves on the right side of the barrier between the initiated and the profane. As the waves of dissemination progress, they spread in widening circles from authorized interpretations and inspired commentaries to introductory guides and, finally, textbooks; thus, as one slides down the scale of interpretations, and the subtlety of the paraphrases declines, the exoteric discourse increasingly tends to focus on basic truths, but, as in the philosophy of emanation, the dissemination is accompanied by a loss in value, if not in substance, and the 'trivialized' and 'popularized' discourse bears the stigmata of its degradation, thus helping to enhance still further the value of the original, and originative, discourse.

Heidegger needs only to affirm that 'philosophy always remains a knowledge which . . . cannot be adjusted to a given epoch. Philosophy is *essentially* untimely because it is one of those few things that can never find an immediate echo in the present',[5] or again, that 'it belongs to the essence of every genuine philosophy that its contemporaries invariably misunderstand it',[6] for all the commentators to immediately repeat: 'It is the fate of all philosophical thought, once it has achieved a certain degree of strength and rigour, to be misunderstood by the contemporaries whom it puts to the test. To classify as an apostle of pathos, an advocate of nihilism, an opponent of logic and science, a philosopher whose constant and only concern has been the problem of truth, is indeed one of the strangest travesties of which a frivolous era could have been guilty.'[7] 'His thought has the appearance of something alien to our times and everything contemporary.'[8]

The relations which are established between the work of the great interpreter and the interpretations or over-interpretations which it *solicits*, or between the self-interpretations intended to correct and anticipate misinformed or mischievous interpretations and to validate authorized interpretations, are very similar – apart form their lack of a sense of humour – to the relations inaugurated by Marcel Duchamp between the artist and the group of his interpreters: in both cases the production comprises an anticipation of the interpretation, and, in the double-guessing game played by its interpreters, invites over-interpretation, while still reserving the right to repudiate this in the name of the essential inexhaustibility of the work, which may incite just as well to accept or reject any interpretation, through the transcendent power of its creative force, which is also established as a critical and self-critical power.[9] Heidegger's philosophy is no doubt the first and the most accomplished of philosophical *readymades*, works *made to* be interpreted and *made by* the act of interpretation or more precisely by the interaction between an interpreter who necessarily *exceeds* his brief and a producer who, through his refutations, readjustments, and corrections maintains an unbridgeable gulf between the work and any particular interpretation.[10]

The analogy is less artificial than it might appear at first: by establishing that the sense of the 'ontological difference' which separates his thought from all previous thought[11] is also what separates authentic interpretations from 'popular', pre-ontological, and naïvely 'anthropological' interpretations (as is Sartre's, according to Heidegger), Heidegger places his work out of reach and condemns in advance any reading which, whether intentionally or not, would limit itself to its popular meaning and which would, for instance, reduce the analysis of 'inauthentic' existence to a 'sociological' description, as certain well-intentioned interpreters have done, and as the sociologist also does, but with an entirely different intention. By positing within the work itself a distinction between two readings of the work, Heidegger finds himself well placed to persuade the consenting reader, when he is faced with disconcerting puns or blatant platitudes, to seek guidance from the master. The reader may of course understand only too well, but he is persuaded to doubt the authenticity of his own understanding, and prohibit himself from judging a work which has been set up once and for all time as a yardstick of his own understanding.

> Here we may show in passing a remarkable example of interpretation mania, calling on the combined resources of the international interpreters' confraternity, in order to avoid the simplistic, as denounced in advance by a magisterial pun: 'In English this term [errance] is an artifact with the following warrant: the primary sense of the Latin *errare* is "to wander", the secondary sense "to go astray" or "to err", in the sense of "to wander from the right path". This double sense is retained in the French *errer*. In English, the two senses are retained in the adjectival form, "errant": the first sense ("to wander") being used to describe persons who wander about searching for adventure (e.g. "knights errant"); the second sense signifying "deviating from the true or correct", "erring". The noun form, "errance", is not justified by normal English usage, but we introduce it ourselves (following the example of the French translators, pp. 96ff.), intending to suggest both nuances of "wandering about" and of "going astray" ("erring"), the former the fundament of the latter. This seems to be faithful to the author's intentions and *to avoid as much as possible the simplist interpretations* that would spontaneously arise by translating as "error" ' (Richardson, *Heidegger* p. 224 n. 29; my emphasis; cf. also p. 410, on the distinction between *poesy* and *poetry*).

The texts are naturally an object of strategic conflict, but their sanctions, their authority, and their guarantees in these domains are only effective if their role is dissimulated, and especially – for this is the function of belief – in the eyes of their own authors; sharing in their symbolic capital is granted only in exchange for that respect for the proprieties which define the style of the relationship to be established between the work and the interpreter, according to the objective distance separating them in each case. It would be worth analysing more fully, in each individual case, what are the specific interests of the interpreter, whether front-line researcher, official spokesman, inspired commentator, or simple pedagogue, according to the relative position that the interpreted work and the interpreter hold at a given moment in their respective hierarchies; and to determine how and where they guide interpretation. Thus one would doubtless find it very difficult to understand a position as apparently paradoxical as that of the French 'Heideggerian Marxists', inheritors of Marcuse[12] and Hobert,[13] if one did not take account of the fact that the Heideggerian whitewash enterprise turned up just in time to anticipate the hopes of those marxists who were the most anxious to be let off the hook, by associating the most prestigious of contemporary philosophies with the *plebeia philosophia* par excellence, then strongly suspected of 'triviality'. Of all the manipulative devices hidden within *The Letter on Humanism*,[14] none could touch the 'distinguished' marxists as effectively as the second-degree strategy consisting in reinterpreting for a new political context committed to talking the language of a 'productive dialogue' with marxism, the typically Heideggerian strategy of an (artificial) *overcoming through radicalization* which the early Heidegger directed against the marxist concept of *alienation* (Entfremdung): the essential ontology which grounds 'what Marx recognized' (albeit in still too 'anthropological' a manner) 'as the alienation of man' in man's most radical and essential alienation, that is his forgetting of 'the truth of Being', surely represents the *ne plus ultra* of radicalism.[15]

We have only to reread the often astonishing arguments whereby Jean Beaufret, Henri Lefebvre, Francois Châtelet, and Kostas Axelos[16] justify the parallels they draw between Marx and Heidegger, to be convinced that this unexpected philosophical combination owes little to strictly 'internal' argument: 'I was seized by an *enchanting* vision – although the word is not strictly accurate – all the more gripping for *contrasting with the triviality* of the majority of the philosophical texts which had appeared in recent years' (Lefebvre). 'There is *no antagonism* between Heidegger's cosmic-historic vision and Marx's historico-practical conception (Lefebvre); 'The common denominator existing between Marx and Heidegger, which links them in my eyes, is our epoch itself, the era of highly advanced industrial civilization and the global diffusion of technology. . . . Ultimately, these two thinkers at least have the same object in common . . . That *distinguishes them from the sociologists, for instance*, who analyse only specific manifestations, now here, now there'[17] (Châtelet). 'Marx and Heidegger both proceed to a *radical critique* of the world of the present as well as the past, and they share a common concern to plan for the future of the planet' (Axelos); 'Heidegger's essential contribution is to help us understand what Marx has said' (Beaufret); 'The impossibility of being a Nazi is part and parcel of the reversal between *Sein und Zeit* and *Zeit und Sein*. If *Sein und Zeit* did not preserve Heidegger from Nazism, it was *Zeit und Sein*, which is not a book, but the sum of his meditations since 1930 and his publications since 1946, which distanced him irrevocably' (Beaufret); 'Heidegger is *quite simply a materialist*' (Lefebvre); 'Heidegger, in a very different style, *continues the work of Marx*' (Châtelet).

The specific interests of the interpreters, and the very logic of the field which guides towards the most prestigious works the readers with the greatest vocation and talent for hermeneutic hagiography, are not sufficient to explain why Heidegger's thought could have been recognized at one point, in the most divergent sectors of the philosophical field, as the most *distinguished* accomplishment of the philosophical ambition. This social destiny could only be realized on the basis of a pre-existing affinity of dispositions, itself deriving from the logic of recruitment and training of the body of philosophy professors and from the position of the philosophical field in the structure of the university field and the intellectual field, etc. The petty bourgeois elitism of the 'cream' of the professorial body which the professors of philosophy constituted, at least

in France (where their origins were often in the lower layers of
the petty bourgeoisie, and where they had shown heroic academic prowess in conquering the peaks of the humanist hierarchy and battling their way up into the topmost ivory tower of
the educational system, high above the world and any worldly
power) could hardly fail to resonate harmoniously with
Heidegger's thought, that exemplary product of a homologous disposition.

The effects of Heideggerian language which appear to be
the most specific, notably all those effects which constitute the
flabby rhetoric of the homily, a variation on a sacred theme
functioning as the melody for the harmonics of an unending
and unremitting commentary, guided by the intention to
exhaust a subject which is by definition inexhaustible, do no
more than carry to an exemplary extreme, and thereby render
absolutely legitimate, the professional tricks and tics which
allow the 'ex-cathedra prophets' (*Kathederpropheten*), as
Weber called them, to re-produce routinely the illusion of
being above routine. These effects of priestly prophecy are
only fully successful on the basis of the profound complicity
which links the author and his interpreters in accepting the
presumptions implied by a sociological definition of the function of the 'lesser ministerial prophet', as Weber again put it:
among these presumptions, there is none which better serves
the interests of Heidegger than the *divine right* conferred *on
the text* by any self-respectingly literate reader. It took a trans-
gression of the academic imperative of neutrality as extraordinary as enrolment in the Nazi party for the question of
Heidegger's 'political thought' to be raised, and then it was
immediately shelved again, as it seemed such an improper
suggestion. Which is another kind of neutralization: the professors of philosophy have so profoundly internalized the
definition which excludes from philosophy any overt reference
to politics that they have finally managed to forget that
Heidegger's philosophy is political from beginning to end.

But formally correct comprehension would remain purely

formal and empty if it were not often a cover for an understanding at once deeper and more obscure, the entente established on the basis of an affinity of the *habitus* and a more or
less perfect homology of positions. To understand is also to
understand without having to be told, to read between the
lines and re-enact in the mode of practice (that is, most often,
unconsciously) the linguistic associations and substitutions
which the producer has initially set up just as unconsciously:
this is how a solution is found to the specific contradiction of
ideological discourse, which draws its efficacity from its
duplicity, and can only legitimately express social interest in
forms which dissimulate or betray it. The homology of positions and the largely successful orchestration of divergent
habitus encourage a *practical recognition* of the interests
which the reader represents and the specific form of censorship
which prohibits their direct expression; and this recognition,
in both senses of the word, gives direct access, independently
of any operation of decoding, to what the discourse *means*.[18]
This pre-verbal understanding is born of the encounter
between an as yet unspoken, or even a repressed, expressive
drive, and its accepted mode of expression, which is already
articulated according to the tacitly accepted norms of the
philosophical field. And Sartre himself, who would certainly
have rebelled against Heidegger's elitist professions of faith if
they had been presented to him in the guise of what Simone de
Beauvoir called 'right-wing thought' (forgetting to include
Heidegger),[19] would not have been able to have the insight that
he had into the expression which Heidegger's works gave to his
own experience of the social world, if it had not appeared to
him dressed in forms fitting the conventions and proprieties of
the philosophical field. Communication between philosophical minds can thus arise from the communion of their
social unconsciouses. One thinks of *La nausée*, where the sublimated expression of the experience of a young intellectual of
'elite' extraction suddenly faced with the *insignificance* (that
is, the *absurd meaninglessness*, as well as the irrelevance) of

the lot which befalls him – that of philosophy teacher in a small provincial town. Placed in an uncomfortable situation in the dominant class, as an illegitimate bourgeois, stripped of his bourgeois rights and of the possibility of even claiming them (an objective situation which finds an almost transparent translation in the theme of the 'bastard'), the intellectual can only define himself in opposition to the rest of the social world, categorized as 'dirty bastards', that is, as 'bourgeois', but in Flaubert's rather than Marx's sense, meaning all those who feel at ease with themselves and secure in their rights because they have the luck and the misfortune not to think. If we agree to recognize in the 'bourgeois' and the 'intellectual' the 'existential' realization of what will later become, in Sartre's philosophically euphemized system, the *'en-soi'* [self-sufficient being] and the *'pour-soi'* [self-conscious being], we will better understand the sense of the 'nostalgia to be God', that is, the reconciliation of the bourgeois and the intellectual ('living like a bourgeois and thinking like a demigod', as Flaubert said), of thoughtless power and powerless thought.[20]

6

Self-interpretation and the evolution of the system

Even if external political circumstances played a part in the prudent withdrawal or calculated dissent which led Heidegger, when he was 'disappointed' by Nazism (that is doubtless by the 'vulgar', insufficiently *radical* aspects of the movement),[1] to adopt topics and authors safely removed in time or acceptable at the time (like Nietzsche, in particular), it is still the case that the famous 'reversal' (*Kehre*), announced in *The Letter on Humanism* and described indiscriminately, as much by its author as by his commentators, either as a radical break or as a logical development, is only the end product of a process of integration engineered by a self-regulating system which, with the help of this supplementary euphemization, adapts itself as if by magic to periods of heightened censorship (under the Nazi regime, after his resignation, and again after the end of the Nazi regime).[2] Once put into practice, the system loses touch with its origins and moves closer to them at the same time: the raw irruption of political phantasms becomes more and more rare as the system becomes perfected and accomplished, closing in upon itself, that is on the ultimate implications of its initial postulates, through its continuous progress towards absolute irrationalism (which was implied from the start, as Husserl had seen, in its philosophical axiomatics, which is homologous to nihilism in politics). Obsessively repudiating any 'anthropological' interpretation of his early writings (particularly in his *Lettre à Jean Wahl* of 1937), Heidegger elaborates a new euphemistics: placing himself under the banner of a spiritual Führer who, like Hölderlin (a sort of Germanic riposte to Baudelaire, who symbolized urban, French corruption), shows the world the way out of its universal decadence,[3] he reiterates his condemnation of common sense and 'ordinary understanding'; he recalls the impossibility for Being-there, 'plunged in negativity and finitude', to escape immersion in the world, 'forgetfulness of Being', 'errance', the 'fall', 'decadence' (*Verderb*): he renews, in terms at once more transparent and more mystical, his denunciation of technicism and scientism; translating into pompous terms the ideology of the *Vates* as it is taught in the grammar schools, he professes the cult of art, and of philosophy as an art; finally he extols mystical abnegation in the face of the sacred and the mysterious, where thought becomes a sacrificial offering, a gift of the self to Being, an opening up, an anticipation, a sacrifice, with the assimilation of *Denken* to *Danken* and the many other verbal games which are as laborious as they are replete with the confidence born of almost universal recognition.

Heidegger consistently gravitated, both through his style and his themes, towards the pole represented by Stephan George – or at least towards what he took George to stand for – as if the recognition which he enjoyed justified him in relinquishing the role of prophetic 'rebel', close to the world and the text, in exchange for the character of the magus of the *Begriffsdichtung*. The source of the process which leads, without disturbance or betrayal, from Heidegger I to Heidegger II, is the work of *Selbstbehauptung*, of 'defence' and 'self-affirmation', and of *Selbstinterpretation*,[4] of self-interpretation, which the philosopher accomplished in his relation to the objective truth of his work as reflected back to him by the field.[5] Heidegger was right to write to the Reverend

Richardson that he had repudiated none of his earlier positions: 'The thinking of the reversal *is* a change in my thought. But this change is not a consequence of altering the standpoint, much less of abandoning the fundamental issue, of *Being and Time*'.[6] In fact, nothing is repudiated, everything is re-negated.[7]

Self-interpretation, which is the riposte of the author to those interpretations and interpreters which at once objectify and legitimize the author, by telling him what he is and thereby authorizing him to be what they say he is, leads Heidegger II to convert into a method the *schemata* of Heidegger I's stylistic and heuristic *practice*.[8] Thus all the later theory of language serves only to constitute as a conscious *choice* the strategies and techniques deployed in practice right from the start: the famous and fêted author assumes his objective truth and renders it absolute by transfiguring it into philosophical choice. If language dominates the philosopher instead of the philosopher dominating language, if words play with the philosopher instead of the philosopher playing with words, it is because word-play is the very language of Being, that is, onto-logy. The philosopher is the acolyte of the sacred, and all his verbal incantations are only a preparation for the second coming (*parousia*).

Here one could cite countless texts where this theme is expressed, especially all the writings on Hölderlin, where we see with particular clarity the political significance of the theory of the poet as *Fürsprecher* [spokesman] – he who speaks *for* Being, that is in its favour and on its behalf, and who, through his return to a primitive language (*Ursprache*), unites and mobilizes the *Volk* whose voice he interprets (Heidegger, 'Remembrance of the Poet' and 'Hölderlin and the Essence of Poetry', in *Existence and Being*, 3rd edn, ed. W. Brock. (London, Vision Press, 1968); 'Poetically Man Dwells', in *Poetry, Language, Thought*, trans. A. Hofstadter (New York, Harper Colophon, 1975)). One should also read *Hebel – der Hausfreund* (Pfüllingen, Neske, 1957) and

R. Minder's analysis of it ('Martin Heidegger et le conserva-
tisme agraire', *Allemagne d'aujourd'hui*, no. 6 (janvier-
février 1967), pp. 34–49). These strategies for the recupera-
tion of objective truth are not incompatible with negation:
'The reference in *Being and Time* to "being-in" as "dwelling"
is no etymological game. The same reference in the 1936 essay,
the reference to Hölderlin's verse, "Full of merit, yet poetically, man dwells on this earth", is no adornment of a thinking that rescues itself from science by means of poetry. The
talk about the house of Being is no transfer of the image
"house" to Being. But one day we will, by thinking the essence
of Being in a way appropriate to its matter, more readily be
able to think what "house" is, what "to dwell" is' (Heidegger,
Letter on Humanism, p. 237; my emphasis).

This work of self-interpretation is accomplished in and
through the corrections, rectifications, clarifications, and
refutations through which the author defends his public image
against criticism – in particular politically based criticism –
or, worse, against all forms of reduction to a common
identity.

One example will show us the extent of his vigilance: 'We
chose the cabinetmaker's craft as our example, *assuming it
would not occur to anybody* that this choice indicated any
expectation that the state of our planet could in the forseeable
future, or indeed ever, be changed back into a rustic idyll'
(Heidegger, *What Is Called Thinking*, trans. F. D. Wieck and
J. G. Gray (New York, Harper & Row, 1968), p. 23). Like the
strategies of imposing caution, the strategies of imposing form
become more elaborate: applying to his early philosophy the
mode of thought that Heidegger I applied to the structures of
ordinary language and to the common forms of representation
of the social world, Heidegger II makes it undergo a second-
degree euphemization, which pushes to the point of caricature
the earlier procedures and effects: thus, in *Sein und Zeit*, the
word *Geschick* comes to be played off (very transparently)
against *Geschehen* and *Geschichte* (*Das schicksalhafte*

Geschick des Daseins in und mit seiner 'Generation' macht das volle, eigentliche Geschehen des Daseins aus [Dasein's fateful destiny in and with its 'generation' goes to make up the full authentic historizing of Dasein]) (*Sein und Zeit*, p. 384, *Being and Time*, p. 436), designating then the 'common fate', the heritage of the whole *people* that Being-there must assume in 'authenticity'; in Heidegger II it is inserted in a completely different verbal combination, as Richardson clearly shows: 'Along with the German words for "sending" (*schicken*), for "history" (*Geschichte*) and for "fortune" (*Schicksal*), the word *Geschick* derives from the word "to-come-to-pass" (*Geschehen*). For Heidegger it designates an event (*Ereignis*), hence a coming-to-pass, by which Being "sends" (*sich schickt*) itself unto man. We call the sending an "e-mitting". Considered as proceeding from Being, the sending is a "mittence". Considered as coming-to-pass in man, it is a "com-mitting", or "commitment" (*Schicksal*). Henceforth, the latter replaces the *SZ* translation as "fortune". The collectivity of mittences constitutes Being-as-history (*Ge-schick-e*, *Geschichte*), and we translate as "inter-mittence". All this becomes clearer in the meditation on Hölderlin's "Re-collection" ' (Richardson, *Heidegger*, p. 435 n. 1).

This passionate, emotive vigilance, which invests a professorial mastery of references and classification in the prophetic enterprise of a search for distinction, doubtless constitutes the true motivation of the systematic evolution which, from one refutation to another, and from negation to re-negation, from expression of distance (from Husserl, Jaspers, Sartre, etc.) to an overcoming of all determinations and all denominations, whether collective or even singular, progressively converts the thought of Heidegger into a negative political ontology.[9]

Those who wonder about Heidegger's Nazism always credit philosophical discourse with too much or too little autonomy: it is a matter of fact that Heidegger was enrolled in the Nazi party; but neither Heidegger I nor Heidegger II are Nazi ideologues in the sense that the Rector Krieck was, although the latter's criticisms may well have inclined Heidegger to keep

his distance from nihilism. Which does not mean that
Heidegger's thought is not what it is, a structural equivalent in
the 'philosophical' order of the 'conservative revolution', of
which Nazism represents another example, produced according to other laws of formation, and thus really unacceptable to
those who could not and cannot recognize it in the sublimated
form given it by the alchemy of philosophy. Similarly,
Carnap's well-known criticism misses its target by attacking
Heidegger's discourse for being vague and empty, a simple,
talentless expression of a 'feeling for life'.[10] In fact a purely
logical analysis is no more able than a purely political analysis
to give an explanation of this dual discourse whose truth
resides in the relation between the declared, official system
indicated by the formal patterning, and the repressed system,
which, in its own way, also provides coherent support for the
whole symbolic edifice. Those who try to insist on sticking
to the 'proper' meaning of the text, that is, a properly
philosophical meaning, thereby granting this emphatic, accen-
tuated meaning the power to eclipse the other meanings suggested by words which are in themselves vague and equivocal,
and especially the value judgements or the emotional connotations which their ordinary usage entails, are in fact insisting
that there is only one legitimate mode of reading, that is, their
own. Thus we see that to gain access to philosophy, to the
strictly philosophical *illusio*, it is not enough to adopt a language, one is also required to adopt the mental attitude which
strives to elicit alternative meanings from the same words:
philosophical discourse can safely be read by anyone, but the
only people who really understand it will be those who have
not only mastered the right code but also the mode of reading
which allows the proper meaning of the sentences to flourish
by placing them in the appropriate terrain, that is in the mental
space common to all those who are authentically engaged in
the social space of philosophy.

Those who impose a legitimate mode of reading, a proper
meaning, give themselves thereby the means of *imputing to the*

listener, to the ignorance or ill will of the reader, the imperfect or improper meaning, that is the censored, taboo, repressed meaning; in other words, they can express themselves without having to declare themselves, and they authorize themselves in advance to disavow any *surreptitious overtones*, anything which can only be interpreted by referring to a forbidden theme. But should we therefore speak of employing dual tactics, or even of deploying a rhetorical strategy? The very activity of analysis, since it objectifies the repressed meanings, tends automatically to encourage such a finalist representation of creative activity. But in fact as soon as one tries to understand, rather than incriminate or excuse, one sees that the thinker is less the subject than the object of his most fundamental rhetorical strategies, those which are activated when, led by the practical dispositions of his *habitus*, he becomes inhabited, like a medium, so to speak, with the requirements of the social spaces (which are simultaneously mental spaces) which enter into relation through him. It is perhaps because he never realized what he was saying that Heidegger was able to say what he did say without really having to say it. And it is perhaps for the same reason that he refused to the very end to discuss his Nazi involvement: to do it properly would have been to admit (to himself as well as others) that his 'essentialist thought' had never consciously formulated its essence, that is, the social unconscious which spoke through its forms, and the crudely 'anthropological' basis of its extreme blindness, which could only be sustained by the illusion of the omnipotence of thought.

Notes

INTRODUCTION: SKEWED THINKING

1 Quoted by A. Hamilton, *The Appeal of Fascism: A Study of Intellectuals and Fascism, 1919–45* (London, Blond, 1971), p. 146.

2 F. Fédier, 'Trois attaques contre Heidegger', *Critique*, no. 234 (1966), pp. 883–904; R. Minder, J.-P. Faye, A. Patri, 'A propos de Heidegger', *Critique*, no. 237 (1967), pp. 289–97; F. Fédier, 'A propos de Heidegger', *Critique*, no. 242 (1967), pp. 672–86; F. Bondy, F. Fédier, 'A propos de Heidegger', *Critique*, no. 251 (1968), pp. 433–7. (1987: this is still true for Victor Farias's book, *Heidegger et le nazisme* (Lagrasse, Verdier, 1987), which, although it relates some new facts, fails to penetrate the work, or enters it only by stealth, giving hostages once more to the defenders of an internal reading: it is hardly surprising that the debate he has unleashed is a repetition of the one that occurred twenty years earlier).

3 The seminar devoted by Heidegger during the winter of 1939–40 to Jünger's *Der Arbeiter* is not even mentioned despite the fact that Richardson's bibliography (W. J. Richardson, *Heidegger, through Phenomenology to Thought* (The Hague, Martinus Nijhoff, 1963), pp. 663–71) was revised and annotated by Heidegger himself (who seems to have refused consistently to give biographical information, through a strategic variation on

Wesentlichkeit, which consisted in establishing thought as the truth and foundation of life).

4 These are principally the appeal to 'German Students' of 3 November 1933, the appeal to 'German Men and Women' of 10 November 1933, the 'Call to the Labour Service' of 23 January 1934 (in 'Martin Heidegger and Politics: A Dossier', *New German Critique*, no. 45 (Fall 1988), pp. 91–114), and above all the 'Self-Assertion of the German University', of 27 May 1933 (*Review of Metaphysics*, no. 38 (March 1985), pp. 470–80). (For original German texts, see G. Schneeberger, *Nachlese zu Heidegger* (Bern, 1962).)

5 P. Gay, *Weimar Culture; The Outsider as Insider* (London, Secker & Warburg, 1968), p. 84.

6 Richardson, *Heidegger, through Phenomenology to Thought*, pp. 255–8.

7 K. Löwith, 'Les implications politiques de la philosophie de l'existence chez Heidegger', *Les Temps modernes*, (1946), pp. 343–60.

8 Heidegger's work faces social historians with a problem quite analogous, although on a different level, to that of Nazism: in so far as it represents the culmination and perfection of the whole relatively autonomous history of German philosophy, it raises the question of the specifics of the development of Germany's university system, and its intelligentsia, just as Nazism raises the question of the '*specifics* of the historical development of Germany', two questions which are obviously not independent (cf. G. Lukács, 'On Some Characteristics of Germany's Historical Development', in *The Destruction of Reason*, trans. P. Palmer (London, The Merlin Press, 1980), pp. 37–92).

9 To these materialists, who are lacking in substance as well as material, we would only recall the truths that they might have discovered for themselves if they had, even once, undertaken a scientific analysis instead of pronouncing magisterial precepts and verdicts (cf. N. Poulantzas, *Political Power and Social Classes*, trans. T. O'Hagan and D. McLellan (London, NLB and Sheed and Ward 1973)), but which they will understand better *in this form*, by referring them to the introduction of *The Class Struggle in France*, where Engels evokes the practical

obstacles encountered by 'the materialist conception' in its efforts to track down the 'final economic causes' (F. Engels, *Introduction* to K. Marx, *The Class Struggles in France 1848–50*, ed. C. P. Dutt (London, Martin Lawrence, 1934), p. 9).

CHAPTER 1 PURE PHILOSOPHY AND THE *ZEITGEIST*

1 M. Heidegger, 'What Calls for Thinking', in *Basic Writings*, ed. D. F. Krell (London, Routledge & Kegan Paul, 1978), p. 346.

2 On the disappointment with which intellectuals reacted to the revolution, see P. Gay, *Weimar Culture; The Outsider as Insider* (London, Secker & Warburg, 1968) pp. 9–10.

3 Cf. George L. Mosse, *The Crisis of German Ideology* (The Universal Library; New York, Grosset and Dunlap, 1964), pp. 149–70, esp. p. 155; E. Weymar, *Das Selbstverständnis der Deutschen* (Stuttgart, Ernst Klett Verlag, 1961); R. Minder, 'Le "Lesebuch", reflet de la conscience collective', *Allemagne d'aujourd'hui* (mai–juin 1967), pp. 39–47.

4 The plot of the film is as follows: in the year 2,000, Freder, the son of the ruler of Metropolis, Joh Fredersen, rebels against the aristocracy which rules over the city and which has condemned the workers to lead an inhuman life underground, beneath the machine rooms. Maria, a working girl, encourages her brethren to expect the arrival of a mediator (*Fürsprecher*) who will unite the city. Freder is this saviour. But his father interferes with his 'mission' by getting the scientist Rotwang to construct a robot which is Maria's double, and which incites the workers to revolt. The plan succeeds and the workers smash the machines, thus flooding their own dwellings. But, meanwhile, Freder and the real Maria have saved the children. Rotwang chases Maria over the roof of a cathedral. Freder follows him. In the struggle between them, Rotwang loses his balance and falls to his death. Moved by the danger incurred by his son, Joh Fredersen repents and agrees to shake hands with the workers' representative.

5 E. Jünger, *Der Arbeiter* (Hamburg, Hanseatische Verlagsanstalt, 1932). Republished in E. Jünger, *Werke* (Stuttgart, Ernst Klett, n.d.), vol. 6.

6 S. Krakauer, *From Caligari to Hitler, a Psychological History of the German Cinema* (Princeton: Princeton University Press, 1947).

7 Heidegger mentions reading the works of Dostoevsky (and also of Nietzsche, Kierkegaard, and Dilthey) as one of the formative experiences of his student life (cf. O. Pöggeler, *La pensée de Heidegger* (Paris, Aubier, 1967), p. 31).

8 Cf. O. Spengler, *Man and Technics* (London, Allen & Unwin, 1932), p. 97 (my emphasis).

9 Cf. E. Troeltsch, 'Die Revolution in der Wissenschaft', in *Gesammelte Schriften*, vol. 4 (Aufsätze zur Geistesgeschichte und Religionssoziologie, Aalen, Scientia Verlag, 1966), pp. 653–77 (1st edn, Tübingen, 1925). (1987: This passage is especially dedicated to those who, through their ignorance of history, are surprised to discover such an *up to date* reiteration of these 'tristes tropiques', which are always present in the intellectual universe, but which are thrown up from time to time on one of the crests of the cyclical waves of fashion.)

10 Mosse, *Crisis of German Ideology*, p. 150.

11 The number of students in higher education rose from 72,064 in 1913–14 to 117,811 in 1931–2, that is, in a ratio of 100:164. 'During the period of inflation, the relative reduction in educational fees provoked an influx of students' (cf. G. Castellan, *L'Allemagne de Weimar, 1918–1933* (Paris, A. Colin, 1969), p. 251, and, on the effects of this influx, F. Ringer, *The Decline of the German Mandarins: The German Academic Community, 1890–1933* (Cambridge, Mass., Harvard University Press, 1969)).

12 Cf. the evidence of Franz Neumann, quoted by Gay, *Weimar Culture*, p. 43.

13 On 'modernist' criticism and its representatives in the university before 1918, Kerchensteiner, Virchow, Ziegler, Lehmann, and especially afterwards, Leopold von Wiese, Paul Natorp, Alfred Vierkandt, Max Scheler, see Ringer, *Decline of the German Mandarins*, especially pp. 269–82.

14 Mosse, *Crisis of German Ideology*, p. 150.

15 M. Weber, 'Science as a Vocation', in *From Max Weber*, trans. H. H. Gerth and C. W. Mills (London, Kegan Paul, Trench, Trubner, 1947), p. 131.

16 Progress through the university was so precarious that both
    students and assistant professors used to say jokingly 'Give us
    another few terms and we'll be qualified for the dole'. As for the
    professors, their material situation had been very strongly
    affected by inflation: thus one of them was led to deplore, in a
    preface, that a mere soldier of the occupying army was paid two
    or three times more than one of the greatest scholars in Ger-
    many (E. Bethe, *Homer* (Leipzig and Bonn, 1922), vol. 2, p. iii).

17 A. Fischer quoted by Ringer, *Decline of the German Manda-
    rins*, pp. 412ff. The actual content of the pedagogical reforms
    suggested by Fischer is very significant: the priority given to
    'synthesis' and to a synthetic, intuitive vision, to understanding
    and interpretation (as opposed to 'observation'), to 'forming
    the character', to the 'training of the emotions', expresses the
    will to impose new models of 'intellectual qualities' and a new
    definition of the 'competence' of the intellectual.

18 K. A. von Müller, *Deutsche Geschichte*, p. 26, quoted ibid.,
    p. 222.

19 H. Güntert, *Deutscher Geist: Drei Vorträge* (Bühl-Baden,
    1932), p. 14, quoted ibid., pp. 249–50. It would be worth fol-
    lowing up Ringer's indications (cf. for instance the declarations
    which he quotes, ibid., p. 214), and trying to identify the com-
    monplaces of academic aristocratism which flourished above all
    in speeches made on official occasions, providing the opportu-
    nity to indulge in a communion of shared dislikes and to engage
    in a collective exorcism of shared anxieties.

20 The brutal irruption of social phantasms is all the more rare as
    the discourse is more censored. It is quite exceptional for
    instance, in Heidegger.

21 H. P. Schwarz, *Der konservative Anarchist: Politik und
    Zeitkritik Ernst Jüngers* (Freiburg, Rombach, 1962).

22 S. Rosen, *Nihilism: A Philosophical Essay* (New Haven and
    London, Yale University Press, 1969), p. 114.

23 Jünger, *Der Waldgang*, in *Werke* (Stuttgart: Ernst Klett, n.d.),
    vol. 5, p. 334.

24 'Let us assume that we have sketched the outlines of the hemi-
    sphere where the continent of necessity is situated. The *techni-
    cal*, the *typical*, and the *collective* are displayed there, now
    grandiose, now awe-inspiring. Let us now move towards the

other pole, where the individual does not act merely in reaction to *"stimuli received"* ' (Jünger, ibid., p. 334). 'In this landscape of work sites, it is *robots* who take control of the centre. This state can only be temporary' (Jünger, *Der Weltstaat*, in *Werke*, vol. 5, p. 502). 'If one wanted to put a name to the fatal moment, none, to be sure, would be more plausible than the sinking of the Titanic. Light and shade clash violently: the *hubris* of *progress* encounters panic, the greatest luxuries dissolve into the void, *automation* disintegrates, in this catastrophic traffic accident' (Jünger, *Der Waldgang*, p. 319; my emphasis).

25   'On the other side, it [the path] descends towards the *lower depths* of the slave camps and the abattoirs where the primitive people conclude their murderous alliance with technology; where one is no longer a destiny but merely yet another *number*. So that to have one's own *destiny*, or to allow oneself to be treated like *a number*, is the dilemma that each one of us must surely resolve in our times, but everyone has to take his decision alone. . . . For, as the *collective powers* gain ground, the *human individual* becomes isolated from the traditional organizations which were formed over the ages, and finds himself on his own' (Jünger, *Der Waldgang*, p. 323; my emphasis).

26   'As for the Rebel, we will use this name for the man who, isolated and deprived of his country by the progress of the universe, finds himself at last delivered up to the *void*. . . . Thus as a consequence anyone is a rebel if, by the law of nature, he is placed in touch with his *freedom*, in a relation which draws him in time into a *revolt against automation*. . . .' (Jünger, *Der Waldgang*, p. 317). 'The anarchist is an arch-conservative. . . . He is distinguished from the conservative in that his efforts are directed at the state of man as such, rather than any particular historical or geographical condition. . . . The anarchist knows neither tradition nor compartmentalization. He does not wish to be requisitioned or subjected by the State and its organizations. . . . He is neither soldier nor worker' (Jünger, *Der Weltstaat*, pp. 534–5).

27   Jünger, *Der Waldgang*, p. 293.

28   'Even supposing that the *void* were to triumph . . ., there would then still remain a difference as radical as the difference between

day and night. On the one side, the path *rises*, towards the *sublime kingdoms*, those realms where life or fortune are sacrificed by the man who succumbs without laying down his arms' (ibid., p. 323). 'The forest is secret. . . . The *secret* is *the private*, the closely *guarded hearth*, the *citadel* of safety. But it is also the clandestine, and this aspect makes it akin to the unusual, the equivocal. When we come across such *roots*, we can be sure that they betray the great antithesis and the even greater identity of life and death which the *mysteries* attempt to decipher' (ibid., pp. 339–40). 'One of the ideas of Schwarzenberg was that one should dive back down from the surface into the *ancestral depths* if one wishes to establish an *authentic sovereignty*' (Jünger, *Besuch auf Godenholm*, in *Werke*, vol. 9, p. 316; my emphasis).

29 'At such a moment (when one senses the arrival of a series of *catastrophes*), the action will always pass into the hands of the *elites*, who prefer *danger* to *servitude*. And their enterprise will always be preceded by *reflexion*. It will at first take the form of a *critique* of the period, of an awareness of the inadequacy of recognized values, and then of a *memory*. This memory may appeal to the *Fathers* and their hierarchies, which were more faithful to man's *origins*. It will tend in these cases towards a *restoration of the past*. If the danger grows, then salvation will be sought more deeply, among the *Mothers*, and this contact will cause a rush of that *primitive energy* which the temporal powers cannot staunch' (Jünger, *Der Waldgang*, p. 326; my emphasis). 'There was always an awareness, a wisdom, superior to the constraints of History. It could only flourish at first in a few minds' (Jünger, *Besuch auf Godenholm*, p. 318).

30 'Whatever one may think of this world of *social security and health insurance*, of factories of pharmaceutical products and specialists, one is *stronger* when one can do without all that' (Jünger, *Der Waldgang*, p. 358). 'The State *levels down* . . . *The Insurance State*, the Convenience State, *The Welfare State*' (Jünger, *Der Weltstaat*, p. 504; my emphasis).

31 'All these expropriations, devaluations, regimentalizations, liquidations, rationalizations, socializations, electrifications, boundary revisions, fragmentations, and pulverizations sup-

pose neither *culture* nor *character*, for the latter pair are hostile to *automation.*' And he continues: 'People are so comfortably ensconced in the *collectivity* and its structures that they have become almost incapable of defending themselves' (Jünger, *Der Waldgang*, pp. 311, 329).

32 'At this stage, one is obliged to treat man as a *zoological being*. . . . Thus we start in the area of brute utilitarianism, and find ourselves close to *bestiality*' (ibid., p. 346).

33 Ibid., p. 355.

34 'This encounter [with a French peasant] showed me the dignity a man earns from *lifelong* labour' (Jünger, *Gärten und Strassen*, in *Werke*, vol. 2, p. 161; my emphasis).

35 '*Recurrent* time is a time which accumulates, and accumulates profits, . . . *Progressive* time, on the other hand, is not measured in cycles and returns, but in scales: it is a homogeneous time. . . . In recurrence, it is origins which are essential; in progression, it is the goal. We see this in the doctrine of paradise, which is placed by some at the origins, by others at the end, of the trajectory' (Jünger, *Das Sanduhrbuch*, in *Werke*, vol. 8, p. 139; my emphasis).

36 Jünger shows quite clearly what was hidden behind Heidegger's play on the words *eigen*, *Eigenschaft*, and *Eigentlichkeit*, that is, to use Marx's terms, 'the bourgeois play on the words *Eigentum* and *Eigenschaft*': 'Property is existential, attached to its holder and indissolubly linked to his being'; or again, 'Men are brothers but not equal'. Jünger's thinner veneer of euphemization is matched by his cruder refutations: 'Which is also to argue that our choice of terminology does not conceal any anti-Eastern [anti-Russian] intentions. . . . We have no intention of mounting an attack on the agents of politics and technology or their supporters' (Jünger, *Der Waldgang*, pp. 378, 380, 331–2).

37 Norbert Elias has analysed the 'network of acquired associations' which these two terms evoke, and which is structured by the opposition between refined social behaviour, elaborate etiquette, and upper-class know-how on the one hand, and genuine spirituality and the acquisition of wisdom on the other (cf. N. Elias, 'On the Sociogenesis of the Concepts "Civilization"

and "Culture", in *The Civilizing Process*, vol. 1, *The History of Manners*, trans. E. Jephcott (New York, Urizen Books, 1978), pp. 1–50).

38 Armin Mohler distinguishes at least a hundred tendencies, from 'German Leninism' to 'pagan imperialism', from 'popular socialism' to 'new realism', while still detecting the obligatory components of a common *mood* in the most diverse movements (cf. A. Mohler, *Die konservative Revolution in Deutschland, 1918–32* (Stuttgart, Friedrich Vorwerk Verlag, 1950)).

39 The interest shown in Hölderlin, notably by the youth movements, can no doubt be explained by his cult of 'integration in a world of fragmentation', and by the correspondence which he shows to exist between a fragmented Germany and fragmentary man, a stranger to his own society (cf. Gay, *Weimar Culture*, pp. 58–9).

40 M. Schapiro, 'Nature of abstract art' (1937), in *Modern Art: 19th & 20th Centuries* (London, Chatto & Windus, 1978), p. 210.

41 F. Stern, *The Politics of Cultural Despair; A Study in the Rise of the Germanic Ideology* (Berkeley and Los Angeles, University of California Press, 1961), p. xvi.

42 Cf. I. Deak, *Weimar Germany's Left-Wing Intellectuals; A Political History of the Weltbuhne and its Circle* (Berkeley and Los Angeles, University of California Press, 1968); Stern, *Politics of Cultural Despair*, p. xiii. One of the important factors of this ideological construction is the eminent position of Jews in intellectual life: they own the most important publishing houses, literary reviews, art galleries, and hold the key positions in the theatre and cinema as well as in literary criticism (cf. Stern, pp. 62–3).

43 Cf. Weber, 'Science as a Vocation', p. 137.

44 Jünger, *Der Arbeiter*, p. 296.

45 Cf. Ringer, *Decline of the German Mandarins*, p. 394.

46 This 'sense of the game' is at one and the same time a 'theoretical' sense which allows one to find one's direction in the space of concepts, and a social sense for finding one's bearings in the social space of agents and institutions – within which trajectories are defined. The concepts or theories are always borne by agents or institutions, teachers, schools, disciplines,

etc., and thereby inserted within social relations. It follows that conceptual revolutions are indissociable from revolutions in the structure of the field and that the frontiers between disciplines or schools are among the main obstacles to that hybridization which, in more than one case, is the condition of scientific progress.

47 The expression was coined in 1927 by Hugo von Hofmannsthal to name a group of people who designated themselves 'neo-conservatives', 'young conservatives', 'German socialists', 'conservative socialists', 'national revolutionaries', and 'national Bolsheviks'. One usually includes in this category Spengler, Jünger, Otto Strasser, Niekisch, Edgar J. Jung, etc.

48 The *völkisch*, as a non-aristocratic elitism which did not exclude the petty bourgeoisie obsessed with the defence of their status, and *anxious to distinguish themselves from the workers*, especially on *cultural* issues, managed to spread to *employees* and affect their principal union, the DHV, which provided considerable funds and encouragement for the publication and distribution of *völkisch* writing (cf. *Crisis of German Ideology*, p. 259), thereby 'romanticizing the workers' view of themselves' and encouraging their nostalgia for a return to the world of the artisan (p. 260).

49 Quoted by Ringer, *Decline of the German Mandarins*, p. 223.

50 Cf. H. G. Gadamer, review of P. Bourdieu, *Die politische Ontologie Martin Heideggers* (Frankfurt, Syndicat, 1975), in *Philosophische Rundschau*, nos 1–2 (1979), pp. 143–9.

51 It is significant that it took the polemics aroused by Heidegger's Nazism for one of the specialists to decide – and, even then, with predictably apologetic intent – to read this book which reveals so much of the truth about Heidegger (cf. J.-M. Palmier, *Les écrits politiques de Heidegger* (Paris, éd. de l'Herne, 1968), pp. 165–293).

52 Spengler, *Man and Technics*, p. 5.

53 Overt racism (one of the features shared by all these thinkers) leads Sombart to place 'the Jewish mind' at the root of Marxism: this association of critical thought and Marxism, which was to lead Hans Naumann to say that 'sociology is a Jewish science', underlies all the properly Nazi uses of the concept of nihilism.

54 Cf. H. Lebovics, *Social Conservatism and the Middle Classes in Germany, 1914–1933* (Princeton NJ, Princeton University Press, 1969), pp. 49–78. This summary presentation of Sombart should not lead us to forget that his work owes many of its properties – here ignored – to the fact that it is inserted in the field of economics. The same would be true of the thought of Othmar Spann (analysed in the same work, pp. 109–38): Spann bases his argument on the priority of the whole (*Ganzheit*), which implies a condemnation of individualism and egalitarianism and of all the ill-famed spokesmen of all the currents of thought stigmatized, Locke, Hume, Voltaire, Rousseau, Marx, Darwin, Freud. Spann's work provides a veritable ultra-conservative political ontology, where the different classes of people are made to correspond to classes of knowledge, and the plurality of forms of knowledge are derived (under cover of Plato) from a sociology of the State.

55 J. Habermas (without indicating his sources) quotes several racist declarations by Ernst Jünger (cf. J. Habermas, 'Der deutsche Idealismus', in *Philosophisch-politische Profile* (Frankfurt, Suhrkamp, 1971), pp. 37–9).

56 Jünger, *Der Arbeiter*, p. 76.

57 One thinks again of the final scene of *Metropolis* where the son of the proprietor, an idealistic rebel, dressed entirely in white, makes the foreman and the proprietor hold hands, while Maria (as chorus, but also as heart) murmurs: 'There can be no understanding between hand and brain if the heart does not act as mediator' (cf. Fritz Lang, *Metropolis* (Classic Film Scripts; London, Lorrimer Publishing, 1973), p. 130).

58 Jünger, *Der Arbeiter*, p. 191.

59 Cf. Lebovics, *Social Conservatism*, p. 84.

60 'The first impression that the type evokes is that of a certain emptiness and uniformity. It is the same uniformity that makes it difficult to distinguish between individuals from unfamiliar animal species and foreign human races. What one notices at first from a purely physiological point of view, is the mask-like rigidity of the face, a rigidity imposed and emphasized by means of external features such as the lack of beard, a certain haircut, and the wearing of tight-fitting caps' (Jünger, *Der Arbeiter*, p. 129).

61 An anecdote recorded by Ernst Cassirer comes to mind: 'To a German grocer, not unwilling to explain things to an American visitor, I spoke of our feeling that something invaluable had been given up when freedom was surrendered. He replied: "But you don't understand at all. Before this we had to worry about elections, and parties, and voting. We had responsibilities. But now we don't have any of that. Now we're free".' (S. Raushenbush, *The March of Fascism* (New Haven, Conn., Yale University Press, 1939), p. 40, quoted by E. Cassirer, *The Myth of the State* (New Haven, Conn., Yale University Press, 1946), p. 288 n. 4.

62 Heidegger, 'Concerning "The Line" ', in *The Question of Being*, (London, Vision Press, 1959), p. 45.

63 Heidegger, speech, 22 January 1934, 'National Socialist Education', in 'Martin Heidegger and Politics: A Dossier', *New German Critique*, no. 45 (Fall 1988), p. 113; my emphasis.

64 Heidegger, 'The Question concerning Technology', in *Basic Writings*, ed. D. F. Krell (London, Routledge & Kegan Paul, 1978), pp. 287–317, especially pp. 310, 314.

65 Jünger, *Der Arbeiter*, pp. 63–6, 90–1.

66 M. F. Burnyeat, 'The Sceptic in his Place and Time', in R. Rorty, J. B. Schneewind, and Q. Skinner (eds), *Philosophy in History* (Cambridge, Cambridge University Press, 1984), p. 251.

67 Palmier, *Écrits politiques de Heidegger*, p. 196.

68 Heidegger, 'Concerning "The Line" ', pp. 41, 45, 47.

69 Heidegger, *An Introduction to Metaphysics* (New Haven, Conn., Yale University Press, 1987), p. 99.

70 Rosen, *Nihilism*, pp. 114–19. (1937: And it is remarkable that we find in the most authentically ontological of the philosophical texts the calculated refusal to repudiate Nazism of which Victor Farias has recently discovered more material evidence, such as the continued payment of subscriptions.)

CHAPTER 2 THE PHILOSOPHICAL FIELD AND THE SPACE OF POSSIBILITIES

1 Since Nietzsche's *Untimely Remarks* put it on trial, people have often drawn attention to the militant apoliticism which forms

the basis of the German academic ethos, and the withdrawal into the cult of the internal and the artistic which it implies. Ludwig Curtius attributes to this social and mental divide between politics and culture the extraordinary passivity which was displayed by the German professorial body, bent on its purely academic concerns, in the face of Nazism (cf. L. Curtius, *Deutscher und antiker Geist* (Stuttgart, 1950), pp. 335ff.).

2 If we need proof of this, we only need look at Heidegger's treatment of Jünger's concepts, like *Typus*, for instance.

3 Cf. J. Vuillemin, *L'héritage kantien et la révolution copernicienne* (Paris, P.U.F., 1954). Jules Vuillemin considers the architectonic structure of the three major 'readings' of Kantianism, and reconstructs a sort of ideal history of their sequence, whose motive force he takes to be negativity, with Cohen negating Fichte and Heidegger Cohen, which would imply a displacement of the Kantian centre of gravity from the Dialectic to the Analytic, then the Aesthetic.

4 F. Ringer, *The Decline of the German Mandarins: The German Academic Community, 1890–1933* (Cambridge, Mass., Harvard University Press, 1969), p. 103.

5 E. Everth, quoted by G. Castellan, *L'Allemagne de Weimar, 1918–1933* (Paris: A. Colin, 1969), pp. 291–2.

6 These features still characterize the philosophical doxa, and thus the probable reception among philosophers in Germany and other countries of a book like this one. (1987: And nothing better attests the persistence of the hierarchical bias adopted by philosophy towards the social sciences than the calculated omission of certain topics by the philosophers, whether Heideggerian or not, who took part in the debate provoked in France by Victor Farias's book.)

7 Cf. H. A. Grunsberg, *Der Einbruch des Judentums in die Philosophie* (Berlin, Junker und Dünnhaupt, 1937).

8 W. Windelband, *Die Philosophie im deutschen Geistesleben des 19. Jahrhunderts* (Tübingen, 1927), pp. 83–4, quoted by Ringer, *Decline of the German Mandarins*, p. 307.

9 G. Gurvitch, *Les tendences actuelles de la philosophie allemande* (Paris, Vrin, 1930), p. 168.

10 Cf. Ringer, *Decline of the German Mandarins*, p. 213.

11 H. Cohen, *Ethik des reinen Willens* (Berlin, Cassirer, 1904),

quoted by H. Dussort, *L'Ecole de Marburg* (Paris, P.U.F., 1963), p. 20 (Henri Dussort notes that this left-wing Kantianism was to find an echo in the Austrian Marxist Max Adler, notably in his *Kant und der Marxismus*).

12 F. Ringer, *Decline of the German Mandarins*, p. 309.

13 To which one should add the capacity, typical of the professor or the *grammarian* (and measured in intelligence tests), to produce or understand simultaneously several *practically exclusive* senses of the same word (for instance the different senses taken by the word 'relation' when relating to a family relation, the relation of an anecdote, and the relation between history and philosophy).

14 G. Schneeberger, *Nachlese zu Heidegger* (Bern, 1962), p. 4.

15 We are aware of the various disclaimers which have been applied to this phrase. Yet if we wish to judge more accurately what support of the Nazi movement implied, and what kind of relations it fostered, we should remember that, however ambiguous the origins of National Socialist ideology may have been (as is often alleged), undeniable signs of its true nature had already been revealed much earlier within the university itself. As early as 1894, Jewish students had been excluded from the student 'confraternities' in Austria and South Germany, although converted Jewish students were accepted in the North. Their exclusion became complete when in 1919 all the German confraternities, as well as calling for a *numerus clausus* for Jews, subscribed to the 'Eisenach Resolution'. Echoing the anti-semite demonstrations which broke out among the students, outbreaks of hostility to Jews or left-wing professors were frequently organized by the teachers themselves, as for instance at Heidelberg and Breslau in 1932. On this decisive point too, the German universities were in the vanguard of the evolution towards Nazism.

16 T. Cassirer, *Aus meinem Leben mit Ernst Cassirer* (New York, 1950), pp. 165–7, quoted by Schneeberger, *Nachlese zu Heidegger*, pp. 7–9.

17 Hühnerfeld recounts that at Marburg Heidegger had a suit made according to the theories of the post-romantic painter Otto Ubbelohde, who recommended a return to folk costume: the suit, comprising a pair of tight trousers and a frock-coat,

was called the 'existential suit' (P. Hühnerfeld, *In Sachen Heidegger, Versuch über ein deutsches Genie* (Munich, List, 1961), p. 55).

18 'When the students returned from the front in 1918 . . ., a rumour soon started to spread through the philosophy departments of the German universities: over in Freiburg, there was not only the ridiculous Edmund Husserl, with his enormous moustache, there was also a young assistant, a man of unassuming appearance, who looked more like an electrician called in to check the wiring than a philosopher. This assistant had an extraordinarily radiant personality' (ibid., p. 28).

19 To fully understand the discreetly anti-semitic overdetermination of the whole Heideggerian relation to the intellectual world, it would be necessary to recreate the whole ideological atmosphere with which Heidegger was inevitably impregnated. Thus for instance the association between Jews and modernity or between Jews and destructive criticism is everywhere present, in particular in anti-Marxist writings: thus for instance H. Von Treitschke, professor at the University of Berlin, famous for his promulgation of *völkisch* ideology at the end of the nineteenth century, accuses the Jews of ruining German farming by introducing machinery into the countryside (cf. G. L. Mosse, *The Crisis of German Ideology* (The Universal Library; New York, Grosset and Dunlap, 1964), p 201).

20 Heidegger, letter to *Die Zeit*, 24 September 1953, quoted by J.-M. Palmier, *Les écrits politiques de Heidegger* (Paris, éd. de l'Herne, 1968), p. 81. This opposition is perfectly common in conservative thought (one finds it for example in Zola's *La débâcle*).

21 The avant-gardism of rediscovery or restoration, notably in the case of poetry, the most academic of the arts, is perfectly suited to the first-generation academic who, being ill at ease in the intellectual world, has turned his back on all the avant-garde aesthetic movements (expressionist cinema or painting, for example) and who finds in the mode for the archaic an avant-gardist justification of his rejection of the modern.

22 As we can see from Cassirer's contribution to the Davos debate (*Débat sur le kantisme et la philosophie, Davos, mars 1929*, p. 25), there is no doubt that it was this rehabilitation of the

everyday which Heidegger's contemporaries found most
striking.

23 F. Stern, *The Politics of Cultural Despair; A Study in the Rise
    of the Germanic Ideology* (Berkeley and Los Angeles, Univer-
    sity of California Press, 1961).

24 W. Z. Laqueur, *Young Germany; A History of the German
    Youth Movement* (London: Routledge, 1962), pp. 178–87.

25 George's style earned the imitation of a whole generation, in
    particular through the intermediary of the 'youth movement'
    (*Jugendbewegung*), which was seduced by his aristocratic ideal-
    ism and his contempt for 'arid rationalism': 'His style was
    imitated and his few quotations were repeated often enough –
    phrases about he who once has circled the flame and who for-
    ever will follow the flame; about the need for a new nobility
    whose warrant no longer derives from the crown or escutcheon;
    about the Führer with his *völkisch* banner who will lead his
    followers to the future Reich through storm and grisly portents,
    and so forth.' (ibid., p. 135)

26 Heidegger explicitly evokes tradition – and, more precisely,
    Plato's distortion of the word *eidos* – to justify his technical
    usage of the word *Gestell*: 'According to ordinary usage, the
    word *Gestell* [frame] means some kind of apparatus, e.g., a
    bookrack. *Gestell* is also the name for a skeleton. And the
    employment of the word *Gestell* [enframing] that is now
    required of us seems equally eerie, not to speak of the arbitrari-
    ness with which words of a mature language are so misused. Can
    anything be more strange? Surely not. Yet this strangeness is an
    old custom of thought' (Heidegger, 'The Question concerning
    Technology', in *Basic Writings*, ed. D. F. Krell, London:
    Routledge & Kegan Paul, 1978, p. 301). Against the same
    accusation of imposing 'randomly arbitrary' meanings,
    Heidegger replies, in 'A Letter to a Young Student', with an
    exhortation to 'learn the craft of thinking' (Heidegger, 'The
    Thing', in *Poetry, Language, Thought* (New York, Harper
    Colophon, 1975), p. 186.

CHAPTER 3 A 'CONSERVATIVE REVOLUTION' IN PHILOSOPHY

1 As I tried to show on the subject of Jacques Derrida's reading of Kant's *Critique of the Faculty of Judgement*, 'deconstruction' is destined to achieve only 'partial revolutions' as long as it does not bring into play *all* the presumptions whose recognition is implied in the fact of claiming the status of 'philosopher' for the author, and 'philosphical' dignity for his discourse (cf. P. Bourdieu, *Distinction*, trans. R. Nice (London, Routledge, 1984), pp. 494–5.

2 It is the choice of the second option which caused me to discuss Althusser and Balibar in the overtly iconoclastic language of the comic strip, to mark the break between the scientific objectification of a philosophical rhetoric, and 'philosophical discussion' (cf. P. Bourdieu, 'La lecture de Marx: Quelques remarques critiques à propos de "Quelques remarques à propos de *Lire le Capital*"', *Actes de la recherche en sciences sociales*, no. 5/6 (1975), pp. 65–79).

3 Given the size of the task indicated, one cannot help thinking that the method itself deserves better than the application that one can make of it, if one is unable to master the whole set of epistemological disciplines (philosophical, historical, political, etc.) which would be indispensable to give it all necessary rigour.

4 As Richardson, who is surely not to be suspected of sociologism, remarks, 'only two problems were *philosophically acceptable*: the critical problem of knowledge and the critical problem of values' (W. J. Richardson, *Heidegger, through Phenomenology to Thought* (The Hague, Martinus Nijhoff, 1963), p. 27; my emphasis). One of the major effects of the field consists precisely in imposing a *specific definition* (philosophical, scientific, artistic, etc.) of what is acceptable and what unacceptable.

5 Cf. J. Vuillemin, *L'héritage kantien et la révolution copernicienne* (Paris, P.U.F., 1954), especially p. 211 and, for this whole analysis, the third part of this book (pp. 210–96) devoted to Heidegger.

6 Cf. Richardson, *Heidegger*, p. 386.

7 Before granting Heidegger the leading role in this debate, as the

'rebel', standing up to the mandarin suffused with bourgeois, metropolitan, cosmopolitan culture, we should remember that, like Simmel, another eminent Jewish intellectual, who was appointed professor at Strasbourg only in 1914, that is, four years before his death, Cassirer was only able to obtain his *venia legendi* with the support of Dilthey, and was appointed professor only in 1919, when he was forty-five, and that in the struggling and progressive new university of Hamburg (cf. F. Ringer, *The Decline of the German Mandarins: The German Academic Community, 1890–1933* (Cambridge, Mass., Harvard University Press, 1969), pp. 136–7), which was also the seat of the *Warburg Institut* which, with Max Horkheimer's *Institut für Sozialforschung* at Frankfurt, threw down a challenge to the old German university system which was more acute, and less easy to assimilate, than that posed by Heidegger and what he stood for.

8 Here too one might say that Heidegger radicalizes Husserl's thought, which, as has often been noted, grants more and more space to temporality and historicity (cf. A. Gurwitsch, 'The Last Work of Edmund Husserl', *Philosophy and Phenomenological Research*, 16 (1955), pp. 380–99).

9 Cf. Vuillemin, *L'héritage kantien*, pp. 224 and 295.

10 To see the specific nature of conservative revolutionary strategy, where two half-turns of the revolutionary wheel bring it back to its starting point, we have only to compare the way in which Heidegger's perspective on *historical tradition* tends towards a restoration of origins, with the way in which Nietzsche's vision of history seeks to overcome historicism by intensifying historicism, and finds in temporal discontinuity and relativity the wherewithal to make a deliberate break and a positive act of forgetting (of the kind which enables one for instance to break free of the static Being of the Greeks).

11 The Janus-like philosopher can exploit this aspect of his thought in order to praise Marxism in the *Letter on Humanism* (1947), in *Basic Writings*, ed. D. F. Krell (London, Routledge and Kegan Paul, 1978).

12 Cf. Heidegger, *Débat sur le kantisme*, p. 46.

13 Following the same logic, Cassirer and Heidegger at least agree to exclude from their debate, which claims to be properly philosophical, all reference to the 'empirical' foundations of

their respective positions (which does not prevent them from supplying a proliferation of objectifying allusions): 'We have reached a point where there is little to be gained from purely logical arguments. . . . But we have no right to stick at this relation, which would grant a central position to *empirical man.* What Heidegger said in the last analysis is vital in this respect. His position cannot be anthropocentric any more than mine can, and, in so far as it does not even claim to be, I must ask: where then lies the common ground to our hostility to anthropocentrism? It is obvious that it is not to be found in the empirical.' Heidegger shows the same support for this implicit axiom of philosophical doxa by refusing to allow the question of the difference between the two philosophers to be 'expressed in anthropocentric terms' (ibid., pp. 46–7).

14 Heidegger, 'Overcoming Metaphysics', in *The End of Philosophy*, trans. Joan Stambaugh (London, Souvenir Press, 1975), p. 109; my emphasis.

15 Even in terms of style, Heidegger seems to have introduced into academic usage, giving it its patent of nobility, *a mystical language and a mystical relation to language* which until then were reserved for the minor, peripheral prophets of the conservative revolution: thus it is that Julius Langbehn, one of the most famous among them, wrote in an overblown style, imitated from the later Nietzsche, constantly resorting to puns, distortions of the meaning of common or proper nouns, and a sort of 'mystical philology' (cf. F. Stern, *The Politics of Cultural Despair; A Study in the Rise of the Germanic Ideology* (Berkeley and Los Angeles, University of California Press, 1961), pp. 116–17; cf. also p. 176 n. 1, the reference to a thesis on the mystical language of the youth movement).

CHAPTER 4 CENSORSHIP AND THE IMPOSITION OF FORM

1 This model is valid for any kind of discourse (cf. P. Bourdieu, *Ce que parler veut dire* (Paris, Fayard, 1982)).

2 Naturally enough, nothing contributes to this more than the status of 'philosopher' attributed to the author, in addition to the signs and insignia – academic titles, publishing house, or quite simply, his own name – which identify his position in the

philosophical hierarchy. To appreciate this effect, we only have to imagine how we would read the page on the hydroelectric power station and the old bridge over the Rhine (cf. Heidegger, 'The Question concerning Technology', in *Basic Writings*, ed. D. F. Krell, (Routledge & Kegan Paul, London, 1978), p. 297), which earned its author the title of 'first theoretician of the ecological struggle' from one of his commentators (R. Scherer, *Heidegger* (Paris, Seghers, 1973), p. 5), if it had borne the signature of a leader of an ecological movement or a Minister of the Environment, or the logo of a group of leftist students (it goes without saying that these different 'attributions' would only be credible if they were accompanied by some modifications in presentation).

3 Thus, while the word 'group' used by mathematicians is entirely defined by the operations and relations which define its specific structure and which are the source of its properties, the majority of the specialized uses of this word recorded by dictionaries – for instance in painting, 'an arrangement of several people into an organic unity within a work of art', or, in economics, 'a set of firms connected by various links' – have very little latitude to stray from the primary sense and would remain impenetrable to anyone who did not have a working knowledge of that sense.

4 Heidegger, *Sein und Zeit* (1st edn 1927; Tübingen, Niemayer, 1963), pp. 300–1, [*Being and Time* (Oxford, Blackwell, 1962), p. 348]. (Page numbers will henceforth refer first to this German edition, and then to this English translation, where possible.) Heidegger was to move further and further down this path as his authority grew and he felt confirmed by the expectations of his audience in the use of that peremptory verbiage which lurks in the background of any discourse of authority. He was to be aided in this undertaking by the work of his translators, especially into French, who were to transform his platitudes and facile neologisms (which were judged more justly by their native readers) into what amounts to a conceptual histo-pathology – which helps to explain the difference between the reception of Heidegger's works in Germany and France.

5 One might object to these analyses that to a certain extent they

only elucidate those properties of the Heideggerian use of language which Heidegger himself expressly claims – at least in his more recent writings. In fact, as we shall attempt to show further on, these bogus confessions are one aspect of the work of *Selbstinterpretation* and *Selbstbehauptung* to which the later Heidegger devotes his entire writing effort.

6 Heidegger, *Sein und Zeit*, pp. 126-7 [*Being and Time*, pp. 164-5].

7 When I wrote this I did not remember in detail the following passage from the essay on 'Overcoming metaphysics' (1939-46) devoted to 'literary dirigisme' as an aspect of the reign of 'technology': 'The need for human material underlies the same regulation of preparing for ordered mobilization as the need for entertaining books and poems, for whose production the poet is no more important that the bookbinder's apprentice, who helps bind the poems for the printer by, for example, bringing the covers for binding from the storage room' (Heidegger, 'Overcoming Metaphysics', in *The End of Philosophy*, trans. Joan Stambaugh, (London, Souvenir Press, 1975), p. 106).

8 *Introduction to Metaphysics*, (New Haven, Conn., Yale University Press, 1987), p. 38. Another symptom of this aristocratism is the pejorative colouring of all the adjectives which go to qualify pre-philosophical existence: 'inauthentic', 'vulgar', 'everyday', 'public', etc.

9 It is obvious that language can play ideological games with devices other than those exploited by Heidegger. Thus the dominant political jargon principally exploits the potential ambiguity and misunderstanding implied by the variety of different class or specialized usages (linked to specialist fields), whereas religious usage allows free reign to a polysemy linked to the diversity of the categories of perception of the audience.

10 One thinks for instance of his discussion of biologism (cf. Heidegger, *Nietzsche*, 4 vols., trans. D. F. Krell (San Francisco, Calif., Harper & Row, 1974-82), especially vol. 3, *The Will to Power as Knowledge and Metaphor* (1987), pp. 39-47, 'Nietzsche's alleged Biologism'), which, however, does not exclude the presence in the system of a sublimated form of *Lebensphilosophie* (in the form of a theory of Being as historical emergence, which, after the fashion of Bergson's creative

evolution, finds its motive force in the God without attributes of a negative theology).

11 Heidegger, *Sein und Zeit*, pp. 56–7 [*Being and Time*, pp. 83–4].

12 We can see the same logic at work in the way in which, nowadays, the priestly–prophetic wing of Marxism uses the 'epistemological break' as a sort of once-for-all rite of passage over the frontier traced in peremptory fashion between science and ideology.

13 G. Bachelard, *Le matérialisme rationnel* (Paris, P.U.F., 1963), p. 59.

14 Heidegger, 'The Anaximander Fragment', in *Early Greek Thinking*, trans. D. F. Krell and F. A. Capuzzi (San Francisco, Calif., Harper and Row, 1984), p. 33.

15 For another, particularly caricatural, example of the omnipotence of 'essential thought', one might read the text of the 1951 lecture, 'Building, Dwelling, Thinking', where the housing shortage is 'overcome' in favour of the ontological sense of 'dwelling' (Heidegger, *Poetry, Language, Thought* (New York, Harper Colophon, 1975), pp. 145–61).

16 This typically 'philosophical' effect is predisposed to be indefinitely reproduced, in every encounter between 'philosophers' and 'laymen', in particular the specialists of positive disciplines, inclined to recognize the social hierarchy of legitimacies which confers on the philosopher the position of *last appeal*, both crowning and 'founding' at the same time. This professorial 'coup' will of course find its best utilization in 'professorial' usage: the philosophical text, which is the result of a process of *esoterization*, will be rendered *exoteric* again at the cost of a process of commentary which its esoteric nature renders indispensable and whose best effects lie in the (artificial) concretizations which lead, in a process neatly reversing that of the (artificial) break, to the reactivation of the primary sense, initially euphemized to render them esoteric, but with a full accompaniment of *cautions* ('this is only an example') designed to maintain the ritual distance.

17 Heidegger, *Sein und Zeit*, p. 121; my emphasis [*Being and Time*, p. 158 translation modified – TR.]

18 J. Lacan, *Ecrits*, trans. A. Sheridan (London, Tavistock, 1977), p. 173. Cf. The Standard Edition of the Complete Psychological

Works of Sigmund Freud, ed. J. Strachey (London, Hogarth Press, vol. 8, 1960), p. 115.

19 Heidegger, *Sein und Zeit*, pp. 127–8 [*Being and Time*, p. 165]; my emphasis. Heidegger's 'philosophical' style being the sum of a small number of indefinitely repeated effects, we have preferred to capture them on the scale of one single passage – the analysis of assistance – where they may all be found together, a passage which should then be reread as a whole, to see how these effects are articulated in practice into a discursive unity.

20 Ultimately, there is no word which is not an untranslatable *hapax legomenon*: thus for instance the word 'metaphysical' has not for Heidegger the sense that it has for Kant, nor for the later Heidegger the sense that it has for the earlier. On this point Heidegger only pushes to an extreme an essential property of the philosophical use of language: philosophical language as a sum of partially intersecting idiolects can only be adequately used by speakers capable of referring each word to the idiolect where it assumes the meaning they intend it to bear ('in the Kantian sense').

21 E. Jünger, *Der Waldgang*, in *Werke* (Stuttgart, Ernst Klett, n.d.), vol. 5, pp. 323–4. (On page 338 there is an evident, albeit implicit, reference to Heidegger.)

22 'Authentic Being-one's-Self does not rest upon an *exceptional condition* of the subject, a condition that has been detached from the "they"; it is rather an existentiell modification of the "they" – of the "they" as an essential EXISTENTIALE' (*Sein und Zeit*, p. 130, [*Being and Time*, p. 168]; see also *Sein und Zeit*, p. 179 [*Being and Time*, pp. 223–4]).

23 Heidegger, *Sein und Zeit*, pp. 295–301 and 305–10 [*Being and Time*, pp. 341–8 and 352–8].

24 Heidegger, *Sein und Zeit*, pp. 332–3, 337–8, and 412–13 [*Being and Time*, 380–2, 386–8, and 464–6].

CHAPTER 5 INTERNAL READINGS AND THE RESPECT OF FORM

1 J. Habermas, 'Martin Heidegger', in *Philosophisch-politische Profile* (Frankfurt, Suhrkamp, 1971), pp. 67–92.

2 Heidegger, 'Building, Dwelling, Thinking', in *Poetry, Language, Thought* (New York, Harper Colophon, 1975), p. 161.

3 M. Halbwachs, *Classes sociales et morphologie* (Paris, Ed. de Minuit, 1972), p. 178. It goes without saying that such a phrase is excluded in advance from *any self-respecting* philosophical discourse: the sense of the distinction between the 'theoretical' and the 'empirical' is in fact a fundamental dimension of the philosophical sense of distinction.

4 It is not the sociologist who imports the language of orthodoxy: 'The addressee of the "Letter on Humanism" combines a profound insight into Heidegger with an extraordinary gift of language, both together making him beyond any question one of the *most authoritative interpreters* of Heidegger in France' (W. J. Richardson, *Heidegger, through Phenomenology to Thought* (The Hague, Martinus Nijhoff, 1963), p. 684, on an article by J. Beaufret). Or again: 'This sympathetic study [by Albert Dondeyne] orchestrates the theme that the ontological difference is the single point of reference in Heidegger's entire effort. Not every *Heideggerian of strict observance* will be happy, perhaps, with the author's formulae concerning Heidegger's relation to "la grande tradition de la *philosophia perennis*"' (ibid., p. 685; my emphasis).

5 Heidegger, *Introduction to Metaphysics* (New Haven, Conn., Yale University Press, 1959), p. 8.

6 Heidegger, *Nietzsche*, vol. 2, *The Eternal Recurrence of the Same*, trans. D. F. Krell (San Francisco, Calif., Harper & Row, 1984), p. 17. The work, Heidegger says somewhere, 'escapes biography' which can only 'give a name to something that belongs to nobody'.

7 J. Beaufret, *Introduction aux philosophies de l'existence; De Kierkegaard à Heidegger* (Paris, Denoël-Gonthier, 1971), pp. 11–112.

8 O. Pöggeler, *La pensée de M. Heidegger* (Paris, Aubier-Montaigne, 1963), p. 18.

9 From this point of view one might connect a certain interview with Marcel Duchamp (published in *VH 101*, 3 (Autumn 1970), pp. 55–61) with *The Letter on Humanism*, with its countless refutations or warnings, its calculated interference with interpretation, etc.

10 The concern for openness, a condition of *inexhaustibility*, is also very evident in publication strategies: we know that

Heidegger published his lectures only reluctantly, in small quantities, and at carefully calculated intervals. This concern never to deliver up a definitive version of his thought was never refuted, from *Sein und Zeit*, published in 1927 as a fragment and never finished, until the edition of his Complete Works which he helped edit, and where the texts are accompanied by marginal commentaries.

11 One might object that this 'claim' is itself denied in *The Letter on Humanism* (pp. 215–17), which does not prevent it from being reaffirmed a little later (pp. 235–6).

12 H. Marcuse, 'Beiträge zur Phänomenologie des historischen Materialismus', in *Philosophische Hefte*, 1, (1928), pp. 45–68.

13 C. Hobert, *Das Dasein im Menschen* (Zeulenroda, Sporn, 1937).

14 See in *Letter on Humanism*, p. 212, Heidegger's rejection of existentialist readings of *Sein und Zeit* or interpretations of its concepts as a 'secularized' version of religious concepts, and his rejection of an 'anthropological' or 'moral' reading of the opposition between the authentic and the inauthentic; pp. 217–21, the rather laboured denial of the 'nationalism' of the analyses of the 'homeland' (*Heimat*), etc.

15 Cf. Heidegger, *Letter on Humanism*, pp. 219–20 [translation modified–TR].

16 K. Axelos, *Arguments d'une recherche* (Paris, ed. de Minuit, 1969), pp. 93ff., my emphasis; cf. also K. Axelos, *Einführung in ein kunftiges Denken über Marx und Heidegger* (Tübingen, Max Niemayer Verlag, 1966).

17 Here we see at work, that is in the truth of its practice, the strategy of 'ontological difference' between Being and entities: can it be a coincidence that it occurs naturally when there is a need to emphasize distances and re-establish hierarchies, between philosophy and the social sciences in particular?

18 It is this blind comprehension that is designated by the following apparently contradictory declaration by Karl Friedrich von Weizäcker (quoted by Habermas, 'Martin Heidegger', p. 106): 'I was a young student when I started to read *Being and Time* which had just been published. I can affirm today, in all conscience, that I did not understand a word of it at the time, strictly speaking. But I could not help feeling that it was there, and there alone, that thought could engage with the problems

that I felt must lie behind modern theoretical physics, and I would today render it that justice.'

19 Cf. S. de Beauvoir, 'La pensée de droite aujourd'hui', *Les Temps modernes*, 10, numéro spécial nos. 112-13 (1955), pp. 1539-75, and nos. 114-15 (1955), pp. 2219-61.

20 To understand the divergence between the later destinies of Sartre and Heidegger we should take into account the constellation of factors which defined the position and determined the trajectory of each of them in two profoundly different fields, and notably everything which distinguished the born intellectual, placed in a false position in the dominant class but perfectly integrated into the intellectual world, from the first-generation intellectual, placed in a false position in the intellectual world *as well*.

CHAPTER 6 SELF-INTERPRETATION AND THE EVOLUTION OF THE SYSTEM

1 Recent historical research tends to confirm this hypothesis which is suggested by the style of the philosophical intention itself, and notably the bias towards methodological extremism which is expressed in it: thus it is that Hugo Ott casts doubt on the reinterpretations which Heidegger was led to give of his relations with the Nazi party (notably his faith in the Führer and his subsequent 'resistance') and shows that his acceptance of the post of Rector does not seem to have been the result of a simple devotion to authority, but that it was inspired by the properly political will to win over the world of intellectuals and scholars to the new ideas of nationalist politics (the Rectorship of Freiburg being the base camp from which he aspired to scale the heights of the Reich) and to become a sort of Rector of Rectors or intellectual Führer. In fact the Nazis, who doubtless were worried by his *radicalism*, did not adopt him, and Heidegger seized on a pretext to abandon his functions (cf. H. Ott, 'Martin Heidegger als Rektor der Universitä Freiburg, 1933-4', *Zeitschrift für die Geschichte des Oberrheins* (1984), pp. 343-58; and also in '*Schau-ins-Land*', Jg. 103 (1983), pp. 121-36 and (1984), pp. 107-30; finally, 'Der Philosoph im

politischen Zwielicht', *Neue Zürcher Zeitung* (3–4 November 1984)).

2 Given the fact that there is general agreement in attributing to Heidegger I *Sein und Zeit*, and the interpretations of it offered by Heidegger himself in *Kant and the Problem of Metaphysics* and in the minor works of 1929, the 'break' mentioned in *The Letter on Humanism* (p. 208) can be situated roughly between 1933 and 1945.

3 R. Minder, 'A propos de Heidegger, Langage et nazisme', *Critique*, no. 237 (1967), pp. 289–97.

4 The word is borrowed from F. W. von Hermann, *Die Selbstinterpretation Martin Heideggers* (Meisenheim-am-Glan, 1964).

5 For an inventory of the principal features of the structural translation of Heidegger's thought, see W. J. Richardson, *Heidegger, through Phenomenology to Thought* (The Hague, Martinus Nijhoff, 1963), pp. 625–7. It is a similar process which changes Jünger's Rebel from the *active and dominant hero* of *Der Arbeiter* to the simple *Waldgang* seeking refuge in meditation.

6 Preface by Heidegger to Richardson, *Heidegger*, p. xvi.

7 For a defence by Heidegger of his political activities under the Nazi regime one can consult his declarations to the armies of occupation dated 4 November 1945 (and also the interview of 23 September 1966 published by *der Spiegel* on 31 May 1976 where he develops very similar arguments: he accepted the post of Rector at the request of his colleagues (notably von Möllendorf, the previous Rector, dismissed by the Nazis) and to defend the spiritual life of the University; he was never guilty of anti-semitism and did everything he could to help Jewish students, etc.).

8 A similar evolution seems typical of the ageing of the productive drive as it becomes academicized and thereby fossilized, by *becoming conscious* of itself through its own objectifications and through the objectifications derived from these (criticism, commentary, analysis, etc.), and by investing itself with the authority which it is awarded, in order to follow its logic through to its logical conclusion.

9 The intent to overcome is also applicable to his own earlier

production (cf. for instance 'Overcoming Metaphysics', in *The End of Philosophy*, trans. Joan Stambaugh (London, Souvenir Press, 1975), pp. 84–110, especially pp. 91–2, on *Kant and the Problem of Metaphysics*).

10 R. Carnap, 'Überwindung der Metaphysik durch logische Analyse der Sprache', *Erkenntnis*, 2 (Leipzig, 1931), pp. 229–33, 238–41.

Index